Single, Sanctified, Satisfied

Blessings as you read.

Evangelist Frances Elbert

EVANGELIST FRANCES ELBERT

ISBN 978-1-64468-146-6 (Paperback)
ISBN 978-1-64468-147-3 (Digital)

Covenant Books, Inc.
11661 Hwy 707
Murrells Inlet, SC 29576
www.covenantbooks.com

I would like to dedicate this book to my dear sister and friend, Sister Theresa Jones who departed this life on December 2019 at the wonderful age of ninety-five years old. She lived a single and sanctified life before many. I salute her for a life well lived.

Contents

Foreword

It is with great pleasure that I have the opportunity to encourage those ladies that are single in the Body of Christ to read this very insightful book by Evangelist Frances Elbert. Her many years of experience as a single sister in the church can be extremely helpful to those who will take the wisdom of her words and the foundation of the Scriptures that she supplied and put them into practice will certainly reap the benefits.

I've known Evangelist Elbert for more than thirty years now, and she has always carried herself with integrity, class, dignity, and respect as a single woman. Her contribution to the Body of Christ is invaluable. I'm glad that God put in her heart to write this book because it can help so many single and (married) people as well. Having been a widower myself, I had to experience being single for a while, so having someone like Sister Elbert as an example can help me and others tremendously.

Her candidness about her past—though painful at times—I'm sure, sheds light on the areas of loneliness and feeling abandoned sometimes by friends and/or relatives because you're not married. There's nothing wrong with them; they are just single and satisfied. Although this book is primarily for single women, single men can definitely benefit from its content. It will uplift and inspire you to be a better man and person that God intended you to become.

Evangelist Elbert, keep the good works going because there is much more ahead, for great is your reward in this life and that which is to come. God bless you in the powerful name of *Jesus the Christ*.

—Apostle Leon Bland,
Pastor of True Gospel Fellowship Tabernacle

Acknowledgments

I would like to use this opportunity to express appreciation to some women who were beyond special to me. They provided great strength and always encouraged me to live my dreams and never give up. They have made their transition from this world, and I miss them so much. These strong and courageous women were my mother, Willie Mae; sister, Celeste; and paternal aunt, Annie. I was encouraged by each of these powerful women to be myself and that I could make it.

In addition to my immediate family, I especially thank my church sisters for taking time to review this manuscript and boosted me in this endeavor. I called this group "Sisters Together" which included: Elisa Brown, Audrey Hicks, Diane James, June Johnson, Tiffany Jones, Sharon Ragland, Tiffany Reddick, Pricilla Ross, and Henri Winters. A special thanks to my sister friend Diane Cottrell who has also been there when I called and especially when asked to review this book at the last minute. Also, to my pastor, Apostle Derek Banks, your wisdom is invaluable. It is my goal that God will be magnified.

Introduction

God has been extremely good to me. It has taken many years for me to stop procrastinating and write what I initially thought would be a magazine article to encourage single women around the world. Well, time has moved on. I have been retired for six years, and it dawned on me that now is the acceptable time. I have been encouraged by others who have published and thought I should add my name to the list among them.

Seriously, my primary focus for this book is to lift the minds and thoughts of my single sisters. Living a free and separated-from-sin life (sanctified) is not hopeless. If possible, I desire to lift your spirits that you move forward in life with a gusto and vigor that only our great and mighty Lord can provide by His divine favor and grace. It is further my hope that all singles will benefit from reading this book, and as you read, the anointing and power of God will touch your heart as He is touching me as I strike each key. If you are not saved, there is still time; accept the Lord before it is too late.

While I do not enjoy telling my age as most women, I am sixty-nine years young with no children and have never been married or, for that fact, even been proposed to. (Wow! I can't believe I have begun sharing such sensitive information so early in this book.) While there are many single women, certainly, I am not the only, first, and definitely not the last in this category. It is important for single women to realize and recognize we each have a path of life that has been designed especially for us. My singleness is complete in the sense that I am unmarried and have no children. Once we really see our lives in a clear and unobstructed manner, we can then become more successful in structuring our everyday events so that we can become not only beneficial but prosperous for ourselves and others.

This book is not intended to get you to become selfish in any way, shape, or form but, rather, to maximize your potential. Take an in-depth look within *you*! As it has been quoted by many motivational speakers across the nation, there is greatness in you, and you must recognize it and act upon it.

I have always loved to teach, and when suggesting to my baby sister, Tiff, of my desire to write a book, for single women, she immediately said that I should make use of the church seminar topics as my chapters. Wow! What a great idea, thus, I am using them. Each of these chapters were seminars where I taught and allowed question-and-answer sessions and where the Lord moved in mighty ways with deliverance. Yes, I would love to come and teach your sisters on any of these or other topics. Knowledge is power, and to paraphrase scripture, address people being destroyed due to the lack of knowledge. This also includes the refusal to accept knowledge when it is given directly or indirectly. There may be times when what I am saying becomes preachy, but I have been called by God to teach His Word, of which I make no apologies.

To all my single sisters that might be reading, be proud of your state of being. Walk with your head high, knowing that you are making a great and fantastic contribution to the well-being of society because you can do much without distraction. Because you are single, you can be that tremendous influencer to many when they are in distress, be that play momma, auntie, big/little sister, or close friend in the time of need. You can do great things with the help of God and belief in yourself.

Blessed to Be Single

The year was 1979. I had relocated from beautiful, sunny West Palm Beach, Florida, to Chicago (The Windy City), Illinois, because my mother was ill, and I felt it was my responsibility to be with her. After all, I was the single female sibling, so who better to be uprooted than me. Not only was I the chosen one, but I was also unemployed due the recent and abrupt cancelling of a federal program to which I was a project director. My world was suddenly changing and totally out of control.

I had only been saved for a very short period; however, now, I had to come to the big city, but I loved my mom, and I needed to be there to see about her care. My brother was residing here in Chicago, but I knew he had a wife and child to take care; my younger brother was in the armed forces; and my sister was married. So the single daughter came without hesitation. In fact, it was God's plan for me to return. I realize that now. God is the architect of our lives, and most times, we have no idea what's ahead—these are the days of our lives; however, how do you choose to live?

Yes, it is a blessing to be single. Single doesn't mean you aren't a whole and complete individual. Colossians 2:10 states: "And ye are complete in him, which is the head of all principality and power." Generally, single women tend to always look at the couples we see around us. Our minds go into movie mode; seeing couples strolling down the street or wherever, we begin thinking we are missing out. Immediately, upon watching those two all hugged up, images begin to form in our minds and usually thoughts go to the natural aspects of male and female physical relationships. It's at this point the enemy begins speaking to your mind; you are missing out on the hugs, kisses, and sexual intimacy. But while all of that is part of a relationship, we don't have a clue if this scenario is genuine or fake, what and how they're really getting along.

First Corinthians 7:34 states; "There is difference also between a wife and a virgin. The unmarried woman careth for the things of the Lord, that she may be holy both in body and spirit…" There is a difference, and it is stated in a manner that lets us know, no sex before marriage. Well, for some, we did not adhere to the abstinence rule until we came to the Lord. There are some women that are yet virgins. It is possible to live a life free of sexual intimacy. Yes, I am single, but it is time to inject this caveat; I did not instantly morph into this mature and responsible single sistah. I am aware of what it feels like to be held, kissed, and caressed by a man. I also admit to knowing the joy and pleasures of sexual intimacy before receiving salvation.

As I write, thinking back to those days, there was guilt in having sex outside of marriage (committing fornication), but when you are not in Christ, you are a sinner and have no power to resist the temptation, you just submit. Your friends are having sex, and you don't want to be left out of the conversations. *No*, not every unsaved person is having sex, but many do. Clearly, scripture uses the terminology unmarried rather than single, but it has the same meaning—being unattached.

To be clear, this book is for those singles who are willing to maintain their integrity. This book is not intended for those that are "shacking" or at a point where they are not ready to refrain. (Okay, I digress) This Scripture lets me know the importance of having the right focus. If our eyes were on serving our Lord and Savior as He has ordained, we would not find ourselves in certain unhealthy situations. Why is it we think there is something wrong with us because we are not married? Why do we, then, allow ourselves to take on the spirit of self-pity and loneliness to the extent we sometimes just cannot make it or stop moving forward with our lives? How many times have you asked God, *Why me? Why am I not married? Lord, is there something wrong with me, if so, show me? Lord, is it my destiny to be "an old maid?"* The questions go on and on in your mind. Let me add, however, that no, I am not a lesbian.

My singleness entails no husband or children. That means when I go out of town, I have no reminder calls to make, i.e. children to do homework or husband to do other things. I used my sick time solely for myself. I didn't have to leave work for an emergency because my precious child had gotten sick or in trouble. Now, I am not putting the duties and responsibilities of parenting down; just informing my single sisters of the lack of stressful days they do/did not have to encounter. Please don't get confused. There, certainly, will be some days in our lives when stress wants to rule, but it was/is not due to children or spouse. I've had to tell some of my married friends they do not have a monopoly on being tired or burnt out. As a single sister, I have certainly overtaxed myself with various commitments that have sometimes gotten the best of me. It is a good thing to occupy your mind with wholesome activities. I'd like to add that I've taken many opportunities to babysit my nephews for extended periods of time. I especially remember having my nephew for a few summers. It was then I really saw the work and responsibility that is required by a parent.

Trust me, I understand the whole biological clock issue, but we must come to grips with the fact and reality that every female will not be able to assist in the procreation of the Earth. You may not be a birth mother, but you can provide nurture and loving attention to your nephews, nieces, and other children within the church and world. Look on the bright side, this is an opportunity to shower your nephews and nieces, as well as the children in church and community a great deal of affection and love. Think about it; you don't have the worry of having to get up in the middle of the night because one of the children is sick. (However, one fantastic asset is you can be available to go in the wee hours of the morning if someone is sick and take them to the hospital. I have done this on numerous occasions and found it rewarding. Keep reading materials handy because emergency room visits last for many, many hours.)

One of the most tremendous assets you can provide is support to your family, church, and community because of being single/free. There are many single parents whom we can assist in caring for their children or serve as a big sister to a troubled child. Just taking them to lunch, shopping, or walking downtown once or twice a month would boost their self-esteem. We are blessed because we have no one to report to or respond to in reference to our life other than Jesus. (This does not include earthly tangible responsibilities to our job, church, etc.)

This book is dedicated to truly single women. If you are a virgin, be proud of this fact. There should be no shame in maintaining your virginity until marriage, and this goes for men also. Our bodies were designed to react to certain behaviors and senses. The way a man touches a woman causes certain reactions, and that is why we do not allow anyone to touch our bodies. The temptation is often greater when you have indulged in a certain behavior. Like a cigarette smoker, if you smoked, it became a habit, and for some you were addicted, and your body craved the nicotine.

The analogy is the same for having been sexually active; the desire to continue will be greater because your sexual desire has been aroused. We were made to experience these feelings, but we must learn how to control them. Yes, there are some things you should abstain from young ladies, and sex outside of marriage is most certainly one of them. As I write, the feelings of shame and remorse have come. No, we do not have to experience everything. Take the advice from others; it will help in the long run. This is where more teaching is needed in our churches by the mothers and responsible missionaries to teach the young woman how to maintain their virginity. It is a struggle, but the conversation must begin before puberty and continue on, so they can be strengthened. The conversation must go beyond what the old mothers told us, "Go take a bath in cold water." That doesn't work! We have a responsibility of teaching our children the facts of life from a biblical and natural perspective.

No, I am not talking to those of you that feel you need to get hooked up/tightened up or respond to a booty call every now and then. I could care less about the man you say you need because he can supply you with some dollars now and then. Is that all you are worth? What are you giving up for those dollar bills? Isn't your integrity, self-worth, or dignity of greater value than a few dollars? Let's be real, there are no freebies in this world.

One of my personal favorite saying is, "You've never read on a death certificate the person died because of lack of sex." However, many have died as a result of the consequences due to having sex—contracting HIV/AIDS is one. Do you really know who they are sleeping with when you decide to allow this man to make a deposit in you without a ring? Is the thrill of a brief sexual encounter worth the trip? Sisters, face the real fact. Sex is not the major focus of marriage, and you will certainly get out of bed to accomplish many, many daily tasks. Don't prostitute yourself in any manner just to have some stuff. If this is your behavior, know that you are labeling yourself as a whore and most people have problems forgetting others' past. How long do you want this badge of identity? *Think about it!* There are yet older women out there expecting a man to take care of them. I say, take care of yourself.

Being single does not mean we should live as a hermit or we are without friends. We should have a balanced natural and spiritual life with a focus that is always pleasing to God. Naturally, we should obtain an education that will afford us the ability to provide for ourselves. I urge all young women to get the best education you can because there are no guarantees you will marry that tall, dark, handsome, and wealthy man. Yes, the husband, according to God, is supposed to take care of the home. What if something happens, and he becomes disabled? Are you equipped and willing to go out and assist in making ends meet until he gets back on his feet? Or better yet, what if his salary does not permit you to live in a manner you are accustomed; are you willing and capable to help?

Financial self-sufficiency has much merit especially in society today. Purchasing a home, your ideal automobile, or traveling should not be placed on a back burner because you are single. Why rent when you can own your home. Owning allows you to have your own personal dirt to plant a garden, sit out on the patio, and just be alone without interruption. Your home can be whatever size you desire and can afford. I recall being asked why I purchased my home being that I'm single. My response was I must have a place to reside, and apartment living was not my cup of tea. Just be aware, if you are kind or weak-hearted, there will be vultures/moochers wanting to move in. Unless you live in a city with great transportation, having an automobile is an excellent means of escape when you "feel like" going. This Earth has some of the most beautiful scenic places, and as a child of God, what's holding you from taking in some of them? Take the plunge; it is not sinful to travel. We are blessed to be able to move at will. It is also good to invest some of your money for the future. Please don't spend it all on shoes and clothes. Ouch! Given your current age and how politics is transforming, social security may not be there.

Be comfortable and get to know yourself. What are your hopes and dreams? To my young readers, just look at life through your own eyes. For once in your life, it is important to be open to what we want without having guilty feelings or remorse. We cannot live our lives as dictated by others. There is absolutely nothing wrong with showering yourself with gifts. Take the time to know "you" because should, when, or if God blesses you with a companion, things will most assuredly change. Don't waste precious time thinking of what might happen. I implore you to live for the moment—a time of life when it is only *you*.

"Redeeming the time, because the days are evil," (Ephesians 5:16). This is an urgent declaration that should encourage you to make the most of your single life in God, as the old folks say, while the blood is running warm in your body. We are in our season of singleness, but it doesn't have to be a dismal and gloomy time. Each season has its unique beauty to the eyes of the beholder. Winter can be mighty freezing and cold, but isn't the snow beautiful when it first falls? The snowflakes lay a beautiful blanket of white snow that covers everything in its path. Sometimes, it snows so hard that the trees, telephone wires, and spaces in the fences are filled with the white stuff. Sometimes, it rains so much that floods happen but what gorgeous flowers afterward. Yes, look at this season of your life as the best and most joyful period that can ever happen. During the fall season, the leaves turn a beautiful and vibrate array of colors that lights up many landscapes. The leaves will fall, but what a show they put on before leaving the stage. This stage of our lives should be the same. We should radiate so that we brighten rooms with our entrance.

Being spiritually single, we can stretch out and commune with God at any time. You can give yourself to fasting and prayer as often and frequently as possible. There will be no one to disturb you when praying or studying. The greatest joy I have learned is being able to bless the house of God and enhance the physical church. I learned something about myself. I can decorate! I am great at home and party decor. As a result, I began making constructive contributions such as decorating the pastor's table on a weekly basis. This became my personal project, and it included purchasing linen, dishes, flatware, stemware, and centerpieces so the table would look festive. The table is always set for four people; therefore, should he and his wife have guests, there are already accommodations present. Afterward, I was granted the approval to decorate our dining hall. This entailed purchasing and hanging various items on the walls.

As time went on, I can say that the Holy Ghost gave me the mind to purchase enough linen, china, etc. so we could have formal dinners for forty guests. I make my boast in the Lord because I was financially able and willing to fulfill this task. When I take on assignments, I did not expect financial support. This is something I personally enjoy. My desire was to do what was necessary to help my pastor enhance the physical church.

Spearheading birthday and other events can be very challenging at times, because once you attach your name to something, it becomes your responsibility, but God has given me the grace to go forward. Being the sole source and executive of your finance is a piece of cake. Single sisters do not have to ask or get permission from anyone on how, when, or what to spend their money. We are free to spend our money as we wish and have no one question it. You can attend unto the Lord as you desire. It is a blessing to give, and God does bless you for your giving.

Single sisters do not have a monopoly when it comes to gaining more spiritual knowledge and wisdom from the Lord, but we certainly do not have the distractions as married or those with children experience. I wished, so many times, I had been taught to embrace my singleness during my twenties. God wants us to set our affections upon Him, and in doing so, we will be blessed above measure. Seeking Him for what He would have us to do with our singleness has to be the focus. There is a place in God we can reach that will certainly enhance our lives and give us tremendous joy. God wants all our attention. Going after Him is a wonderful adventure. It is just you and God. God will not get jealous or tired of you spending so much time with Him. He will not complain and say you are pestering Him too much or too often. Yes, dig deeper and embrace His words. Allow the Holy Ghost to flood your soul every opportunity possible. We can never get too much Jesus. Go after the Lord with as much vitality as you can, and do not allow anyone to stop you. (God does everything decently and in order, so don't try to go where He is not taking you.)

Get in position to speak words of comfort to other single young ladies. (This is preparation time.) Let them know they can and should live a positive life full of joy, peace, and happiness. My dear sisters, there is so much we can gain by learning to appreciate such a precious time of life. Our glass is neither half full nor half empty but, rather, filled to the brim with joy and happiness just waiting for us to tap into. Let's dive into this great, blissful time of singleness with all our hearts.

Once we focus, we should rest in Him. No, I do not mean to lie down and do nothing but, rather, to rest and learn what direction God wants you to take in your single life that will be a blessing to others. When you are resting in the Lord, it is walking in His Word with strong confidence and reliance in God. You have established a relationship with Him. During this stage, you should know the voice of God and move at His command. Having a relationship means you have had some encounters with God and are accustomed to His voice. It is also during this stage that you are learning God more as He uses you spiritually. We are commissioned to be living epistles, letting our lights shine. The only way people will see our lights is by doing something constructive. We can also be on twenty-four-hour call to those that are in need. Stay ready and flow in the spirit.

No, there is nothing wrong with you. You have a mission from God that He wants you to do with joy. You are blessed because you have no distractions; therefore, you are without excuse in your moving forward. One of the definitions for blessed is "bestowing joy, bringing happiness." Yes, you are blessed. You are filled with happiness and joy of being saved and spreading happiness and joy to others at any time. Make sure you are walking worthy because others are watching. Have you thought about starting a "single group?" Begin mentoring preteens and teenagers; trust me they need a place to come and just talk.

Single and sanctified sisters, let us not get caught up in this new-aged notion that "we do not need men." Let's look at it in a proper perspective. God made man to be the head, but this does not mean any and every man is over you. Let me note here that our pastors are our spiritual leaders, but they do not dictate our lives. It is important that we keep things in their proper perspective.

I don't know if this is the place to say it, but some pastors and other males in the church will not allow "sisters" to minister as God has anointed them in the church. Sisters have a place in the ministry and, certainly, should be allowed to flourish as God uses them. First Corinthians 7:34b states, "The unmarried woman careth for the things of the Lord, that she may be holy both in body an in spirit." God has ordained each of our lives to go in a certain manner." Looking at Scripture in Proverbs 31:10: "Who can find a virtuous woman? For her price is far above rubies."

Sisters of God, you have many virtues that can be used within your local church and community, but you must be aware of them. Once we come to God, it is our job to learn what His will is for us. You must stop looking and listening to those other voices. We are not commodities that should be handled any kind of way. My sisters, take care and keep your spiritual ears open. Do not allow "church brothers" to captivate you with flattery and flowery words. Be mindful of people that would like to take advantage of you just because you are single. Yes, there are some "church folks" that will slide up and whisper in your ears. Be wise in loaning your money or allowing people to take advantage of you. It is permissible to say *no*.

Our pastors are *not* our husband, man, or father and, therefore, not responsible for our natural lives. We must learn how to take care of ourselves and not lean on others. There comes a point in our sanctified life where we must put our total trust in God and not look for support from others. (For those whose father is alive, feel free to lean on him if he allows.) My pastor loves his flock and will assist members with finances to get to and from church services and even assist in other areas. This is a great blessing because some churches will not provide this resource. However we should take care not to lean and depend on others. God is rich; let's try trusting Him.

Single does not mean helpless. Learn how to take care of your bills and other business. We must learn to stand on our own. If you do not have a father or natural brother to provide advice in certain matters, ask God to direct you to a male figure who can provide direction and insight. (Now, don't get attached to the brother and start thinking this is your husband. We must watch our flesh.) It is great to have a competent male you can get advice from.

I am reminded that before my credit union established an automobile purchasing program, I would have a brother from the church accompany me to car dealerships. I always purchased new cars, but there were some questions I didn't know to ask nor did I have that price negotiation skill. Some car salesmen operate differently with women versus men. I adopted a "church dad" who I could call upon when things happened to my home; i.e. furnace going out, pipe bursting, or other simple house repairs that were needed. God blessed me with a single male neighbor that has been a tremendous blessing. My neighbor provided major support during my kitchen renovation, driveway paving, and shoveled my sidewalks during winter. Each of these males were always respectful of me, and

I also presented myself in a respectable and sanctified manner. Yes, we need positive men in our lives.

We should know how to cook and clean and take care of household responsibilities but so should men. Don't look at yourself solely as a housemaid or commodity. All of us will not be in the church's kitchen either. We can do other things to further the Gospel. You should keep your body and environment clean. Our bodies should always smell good. Our bodies are the temple of God therefore it is imperative that we keep our bodies clean. Sisters and brothers, watch your personal hygiene. God does not have stinky people. (There are some things which should not be dressed up, and this is one such area.) If you have a medical problem, actively seek a remedy, but you still must recognize and take action. (I digress, but it is offensive and embarrassing to come in public in these conditions. What do you think the unsaved are saying?)

This does happen in the church and must be addressed. Under the law, the priest could not enter the temple until he cleaned (washed) himself. We should not come from our residence with unclean body or clothing. We don't want to bring a reproach upon the church. Your home or apartment should be kept clean as well. Don't let the dishes pile up in your sink and you are inviting guest over. Visitors should not smell bad odors when they visit. Take care of what God gives you so He can bless you with more. If you are not taking care of your studio apartment, please stop asking for a five-bedroom home.

Now, if God has called you into the ministry, do the work of Him that has sent you. Preach and teach the Word in and out of season. Isaiah 55:6 states, "Seek ye the Lord while He may be found, call ye upon Him while He is near:" God can be so close to us that we fail to recognize or feel His presence because of being so preoccupied with other matters. What other things is God directing you toward? Can you see the forest despite the trees? Are your eyes really open? This is your state of being for now, so take the time to appreciate it to the fullest. Acknowledge the presence of God when He wakes you during the wee hours of the morning. Yes, God is moving in your life, but there is more. Seek Him for the more. Remember, you must remember to stay humble, because it is God that is using you by His spirit.

2

Sanctified

Believe it or not, my initial thought wasn't to include "sanctified" as a separate chapter until I was driving one day and heard some very disturbing commentary on a Christian radio station. So let's begin by defining the word "sanctify" which means "to be set apart to a sacred purpose or in religious use [consecrate]; and to free from sin [purify]." Therefore, one that is sanctified would be an individual who has changed their way of living that does not involve doing sinful things. We have been set apart for the use of the Lord while living in a sinful world.

Romans 3:24 says, "For all have sinned and come short of the glory of God." We are not continuing to live in sin but live a life according to the biblical principles of Christ. A sinner continues to sin every day without any hesitation; however, a saint refrains from sinning daily. The devil is, by no means, treating us well at any time. The devil will never stop trying to get us to join his family and sin. There will be times when we might make a mistake, but saints do not just continue doing wrong. We have been set apart from the sinful aspects of the world by the renewing of our minds. We have become a new and changed woman in Christ Jesus. The sinful things we did, we no longer desire to do them anymore. The Word tells us emphatically in I Peter 1:18: "Be ye holy for I am holy." Remember, we are now followers of Christ.

Some of you may not agree with me, but someone or a life experience ran you into the arms of Jesus. There is no shame in acknowledging you got saved for whatever reason. We all have a story of how we were delivered from the clutches of the devil. The soul belongs to God, and when we hear the call of God to receive salvation, it is important that we answer with a yes. There are some that have not given God the yes and as a result life situations are getting the best of them. To make matters worse, the devil beats you to a pulp and yet you remain in his army. I hope you are one of those that answered with a yes and can now testify that you are free indeed from the bondage of sin. Praise God for answering the call because some did not make it and are now in hell.

Living a sanctified life is not a game. I remember, as a child, singing in a circle the Hokey Pokey. You put your right hand in, you take right hand out, you put right hand in, and you shake it all about, and it goes on until, finally, you put your whole self in then out and shake it all about and culminate by doing the hokey pokey. Well, sanctification is a way of life. You are either in or out. There is no middle ground. In fact, Scripture tells that Jesus would rather you be hot or cold and not lukewarm. Sanctification is a life of being sold out and committed to Jesus Christ.

During biblical times, the priests were instructed to wash and purify themselves (outward) prior to coming to Him. There were rituals they had to follow, but now, we live under grace and truth. John 17:17 states, "Sanctify them through thy truth: thy word is truth." The only way we can come to Christ is by the Word. Once we come into that ark of sanctification, we are set apart/separated from the world. No, we are not living in a bubble, but we no longer engage or desire the activities and lifestyles of our past. The bars/lounges and parties we use to frequent are no longer interesting or a part of our life. We put away the Vegas mentality of "what happens in Vegas stays in Vegas." God sees and hears everything and guess what, everything is being recorded. Our entire lives' repertoire changes when we say, "Yes, I believe." We look forward not only to Sunday church services but the weekly teachings also. Prayer meeting is a great blessing because we know God is going to be within our midst. Choir rehearsal is joyful as well as other aspects of working in the house of God with the other saints.

Music is great for enhancing services, but we must hear the Word which is the Gospel of Jesus Christ. Hebrews 4:12 declares, "For the Word of God is quick, and powerful, and sharper than any two-edged sword, piercing even to the dividing asunder of soul and spirit, and of the joints and marrow, and is a discerner of the thoughts and intents of the heart." If you really listen to the Word as being preached by a holy vessel, your heart will be touched. The Word is supposed to stir you and, yes, upset you. Your conscience has told you that certain behaviors are wrong, and you have felt uncomfortable when performing them, but you have conditioned yourself to override the spirit of God. Now, if you yield to the spirit of truth—the truth that lying, stealing, fornicating, gossiping, drinking, drugs, etc. are wrong—and submit yourself to God, you can receive the help needed to stop all those evil devices. Yes, I do mean you can stop completely and never return to them again. Hebrews 4:16 ushers us by declaring, "Let us therefore come boldly unto the throne of grace, that we may obtain mercy, and find grace to help in time of need."

Living a sanctified and single life identifies you by outsiders as an oddball. You no longer fit among your friends, coworkers, and even family members. But I am here to say that it is good being the oddball. The changes in your dress and behavior are foreign to those on the outside. They do not understand why you have decided to alter your way of living so drastically. I am willing to share that as a sinner, I enjoyed wearing miniskirts. In fact, I often comment that I put mini in mini and was showing a lot of flesh. Mind you, I was not fat at the time but very well proportioned. Anyway, while dressing in a provocative manner, I was not really trying to get attention of men; I just wanted to look "fine." When men would whistle and make comments, believe it or not, I was not pleased. It wasn't until I got saved that I really recognized the signage I was displaying and possible messages others were perceiving.

Coming to Jesus removes us from darkness and places us into His marvelous light. Initially, some people will shun you, but they know that your difference and oddness is really a positive energy force in their midst. When things begin to go wrong, they call on you to pray. They marvel that you are maintaining your lifestyle, and I believe behind closed doors are glad.

Matthew 5:16 states, "Let your light so shine before men, that they may see your good works, and glorify your Father which is in heaven." Our light is adhering to doing exactly what the Word of God tells us to do. It clearly lets us know we cannot lie. No, we cannot tell a white/black or multicolored lie nor one for Pete's sake. No, I am not lying on my income tax, so I can get a greater return nor I am going to change my dress because my other "church associates" says their pastor approves certain unholy attire. We were called to be saints.

Scripture uses the word Christian only once, and it was as a means of ridicule because they were called Christ-tians. They were followers of Christ. The world and non-followers knew the saints because of their behavior and dress. Do you remember Peter? Jesus told him before His crucifixion that he would deny Christ. (This was prior to him receiving the baptism of the Holy Ghost.) The maid pointed him out, but Peter said, "I know not the man," and began to curse. Peter was afraid. Today, we do not have to fear acknowledging we are a part of the body of Christ. Are you aware of the real reason Christ came and sacrificed Himself for mankind? The ultimate reason was to redeem man back to His Father, God, and provide an avenue for us to live as He originally designed. Jesus Christ is our advocate, and should we falter/fall, we can go to Him and repent of that sin we committed, and He will forgive.

Praise the Lord that saints especially in America are not being killed for affirming we are sanctified. We can boldly acknowledge being born again and washed in the blood of Jesus Christ. It is a joy to know we can have a meaningful relationship with the one that suffered and bore our sins upon Him. It is because He rose from the dead that we can enjoy these great Holy Ghost pleasures. The joys of living for God are truly undeniable and unspeakable to someone on the outside. Our language has no words that can adequately describe the life of one who has given their life to Christ. Psalm 19:9–10 sums it up: "The fear [love] of the Lord is clean, enduring forever: the judgements of the Lord are true and righteous altogether. More to be desired are they than gold, yea, than much fine gold: sweeter also than honey and the honeycomb."

Sanctified sisters, we must stand as never before. The devil is waging a full battle against the body of Christ with all kinds of ammunition. He is saying we can go anywhere, do anything, dress any way, and that once we come to Christ, we are in for life. The latter is the biggest lie ever told. If you are not walking according to the Word of God, your name is removed from the Book of Life. John 8:44 is clear: "Ye are of your father the devil, and the lusts of your father ye will do. He was a murderer from the beginning, and abode not in the truth, because there is no truth in him. When he speaketh a lie, he speaketh of his own: for he is a liar and the father of it." Therefore, if one is walking in dishonesty, lusts of flesh, and other sinful behaviors, they belong to the devil. However, you are a child of God if you've made the change, submitted yourself, and remained committed. Watch and stay on guard. Take care that the devil doesn't use you.

Remember, he is very cunning and crafty and will use a saint in matters if we are not careful. The Scripture above clearly lets us know that the devil is a liar. Why would you believe a liar? If you know a person is a habitual liar, anyone thinking right would certainly not believe anything they reported. Now, with that in mind, why would you believe the devil when he comes with a truckload of lies that tickle your ears? The devil is constantly looking for souls to go to hell with him. Think first and then respond. Sometimes, it is best not to respond, just keep living the life.

So, there is nothing wrong in declaring you are sanctified when asked. Yes, living free and separated from sin is a life of joy, happiness, and peace. You are not doing this on your own accord but with the help of God. You no longer must yield to the works of the flesh. You will be cleaner than Ivory soap. Once we come to Jesus according to Hebrews 10:17, "And their sins and iniquities will I remember no more," we can walk proudly. Once we accept Christ as our Savior, we will be equipped to maintain the life, but you must be taught how to use each piece of equipment, and it will take time, but you can *win*.

Living a sanctified life is not without trials, tests, and persecutions, but we have the peace and power of God within to help us through those difficult situations and circumstances. We do not have to holler or have a tantrum. Just trust in the Lord for strength to endure. There are many times when we don't have to open our mouths because God will resolve the situation. We do not have to fight battles when lied upon. We just live knowing the devil has nothing in us. We do not walk around with hatred in our hearts, carrying a grudge against someone, or just being unforgiving. Oh, yes, we love our enemies. Now, we are not just going to sit and allow people to take advantage of us. Correct them, but do it in a respectful manner. Kind words turn away wrath. Trust me, it works. God fights our battles.

It is a great joy to live this fantastic and joy-filled life. A life where you feel the joy of the Lord in your soul that causes you to say, "Thank You, Jesus, for saving me." The flood of immense emotion comes when you know your life is pleasing God. I can and do live a sin-free life. Saints are living free and separated from sin. Now, let me help you out. There might be something that we are not aware within us, but once we notice/hear and it is brought to light, we should renounce it immediately. A life that was instituted years ago and made ultimately possible by Jesus coming and bearing all our sins upon Him because as stated in John 3:16, "For God so loved the world, that He gave His only begotten Son, that whosoever believeth in Him should not perish, but have everlasting life." Oh, the natural body made of clay will one day die, but the soul will, for all eternity, be with Jesus.

We are living in the last days. You can see every minute of the day the signs of evil men getting worse and worse with no remorse for the awful acts they perform. We must be that uncompromising beacon of light letting sinners know that living a sanctified life is doable. We cannot be wishy-washy and double-minded. We can stand and be unmovable in the ways of holiness. Holiness has not changed over the thousands of years, and certainly, in our limited time on Earth, we can remain steadfast. No doubt, someone is watching you daily to see if you will slip and go back. Do not give the devil the satisfaction. He wants you to go with him, but remember, he is the father of lies. You can make it.

We must remember that we have been equipped to maintain this way of living. We must keep on the armor of God 24/7. It doesn't matter what comes against us; we can endure and be victorious.

Thank God, I am sanctified and proud of it.

3

"Spirits! You Stand Your Ground"

I am beginning this chapter with a Scripture because I really need to get my preaching on for just a few lines. "Be sober, be valiant; because your adversary the devil, as a roaring lion, walketh about, seeking whom he may devour" (1 Peter 5:8). The devil is after everyone that doesn't belong to his camp, and we are prime candidates. The devil looks for weaknesses, especially in our conversations. Sometimes, without thinking, a person will ask why you aren't married. Even the church folks will ask this question knowing that Scripture says, "Who so findeth a wife findeth a good thing, and obtaineth favor of the Lord" (Proverbs 18:22). Now, this lets you know the ownership/responsibility/charge is not on you but the man. It is our responsibility to live godly and soberly and be in a place to be found. Of course, when someone says this, it triggers all kinds of responses. Just get to the point of saying, "I have not been found yet."

We cannot allow the spirit of "I've got to have a man" enter our spiritual mind. There was a play years ago where the female character was in wanton and proclaimed she would take any man which would include: the garbage man, cameraman, policeman, fireman, and on and on. That spirit will push you into positioning yourself before the single brothers in your church or job. We stand on the promises of God and not man. Do not let anyone tell you that you must have a man.

Human man does not and cannot give you life. God promised to give us life and that more abundantly; however, it does not read a husband being a specific inclusion in the abundance. (If God doesn't do it, you will be depleted of joy, peace, happiness, etc.) It is so imperative that we do not let the flesh get the best of us. The only man we should allow into our lives is the one God has ordained specifically for us. Don't permit just any brother to come with his smooth words, claiming to be the one. God has given us an insight and intuition to know and sense when something is not right. Follow that. Don't be moved when a sister encourages you to fall for his conversation of flattery or what he might possess. Don't be so easily moved by compliments.

I recall being in the line for breakfast one Sunday. This "brother" comes up and says, "You look so nice." My reply was thanks, and that's it. Now, the sweet sister behind me says that was so nice of him. I agreed with her but added that I knew how I looked before leaving home. Unbeknownst to her, this "brother" was a stalker. I finally had to go to the pastor regarding his behavior. There are certain things we do not have to accept, and I have no problem putting you in your place if you are wrong. We must watch out for those "brothers" that think they can push up on you because you have some things already in place. (I'm talking about job, house, car, etc.) My declaration continues to be I will not be paying for the engagement ring, his tuxedo, and wedding; and then, he comes only with his clothes that are in a plastic bag. The devil is a lie. Do not sell yourself short. Come on, you cannot be that desperate.

I do not recall the date, but I realize, as I write this book, that I had put up an invisible wall. This wall said, "HOLY GHOST ON GUARD, DO NOT ENTER," and did not allow me to be unduly impressed by men that did not mean me any good. I established a mannerism in such a way that I would not permit myself to be tricked by the devil. Flattery is something men use to gain your confidence and get some women to get giddy, but did you not look in the mirror before you left home. Now, I am not saying to refuse a compliment, but don't get carried away. There is a way in which you carry yourself that some will say she thinks she is better than anyone else. Others might say she is bossy and acts so uppity, when that is not you in the least. Sometimes, a sister's confidence is perceived by others in a very negative way. I am who I am by the grace of God, and I am not willing to condescend to a lesser degree because you are uncomfortable with who God has made me to be. I am not talking sisters being haughty; we should stay in our place of meek and humbleness which is required for the brothers also. Let the church say, "Amen to that."

We must be mindful of some triggers, alert ourselves, and become watchful that we do not begin to entertain those spirits. Here are a few that I would consider common ones: watching romantic movies, constant company with married friends especially around wives that are always hugging and kissing in your presence. (I am not saying the wife should not do those things, but sometimes, depending on the situation, they should be mindful of a single sister's presence and show respect). Attending bridal showers, weddings, and baby showers are also significant events that will set and send our emotions into a full-blown major movie epilogue.

As a defense, get a certain Scripture, prayer, or song that you can openly recite upon arrival to your home, so you won't get caught up in the "woe it's me syndrome." Don't yield to the spirit of self-pity and loneliness and no-one-wants-me. Just think, *I am a rare gem, and it is taking Mr. Brother Right time to first locate my whereabouts before he can begin righteously obtaining such a precious gem as I.* He will only be able to locate you once he is in the position God wants *him to be and, likewise, so are you. Use this time to become more spiritual.*

"And they that are Christ's have crucified the flesh with the affections and lusts" (Galatians 5:24). Crucified means to kill it. Make sure the flesh is dead. Okay, be serious, I am not telling you to commit suicide but, rather, to give up/cast down those things of flesh that you know are against God. Yes, this includes masturbation. I don't care what the doctor, your friend, or anyone else tells you; this is against God. This is self-gratification, and God does not approve. The devil will tell you to console/satisfy yourself. So you want to replace your former boyfriend with your hand or some other object. I mentioned in another chapter that you are not going to die because you are not sexually active.

Now, as we discuss spirits, you must recognize that God is working on you. There are times when we must get back on the potter's wheel for a makeover in order to meet God's specifications. Yes, somewhere along the line of life, we got in the wrong lane. Yes, there are some impurities and imperfections that need to be worked out of you. In order to mature in God's wisdom and knowledge, we must be put to the test. God knows our position in Him. We are not sure; therefore, we must be tried in many ways. There will be flashbacks from events of our past life. When this happens, how will you react? Do you think this is a sign to return to that old creature? Your response should be no. It is at this point you should recognize this is the devil seeking your attention.

Fight the good fight of faith by occupying yourself with projects and committee work. Now that I am retired, I pray more because the enemy wants me to change my focus and think on things that are nonproductive. Sometimes, I have been so active with a myriad of events that once I arrive home, I immediately fall asleep. I am, sometimes, so busy I want to take a break, but my projects keep me occupied with planning for the next event. Colossians 3:2 instructs us to "set your affection on things above not on things on the Earth." So this lets us know not to think on the temporal things, especially those that we have *no* control over. I have found a love for cooking and baking that I never knew I had, so again, there are days I am trying new recipes, I must say, with great success. Much of what I cook or bake is shared with others. (I generally prepare very large quantities of dishes.)

I met the love of my life the summer of my senior year of high school. He was two years older and a recent high school grad from a nearby school. He was the friend of my best friend's boyfriend. Yes, he was my first real boyfriend, and of course, I immediately fell in love. I remember walking down the middle of the street holding his hand. This was a no-no back in the day. I was hoping my mother did not come out of the house and see this because I would be in for a tongue lashing. No, I was not caught. He came to the house, and I introduced him to my mom with no hesitation. We began dating and because I was "green" not knowing many things, I thought I was his one and only. There were times when he promised to come and take me out but never showed up.

Yes, I patiently waited and waited for hours. When he did come, usually a day or so later, he had some story that I, of course, accepted. Well, as I began my senior year of high school, he enlisted in the marine corps and was soon off to Vietnam. I promised to write him at least once a week. Once he left, I began having fainting spells from out of nowhere, soon to only learn that I was pregnant. How can this be, I'm only seventeen years old, and there is no way I want to drop out of school. I do not want to be labeled like "those other girls." My dream of getting married and having children is now out of the window, and how am I going to tell my mom?

In one of my weekly letters scented with perfume, I told him of my pregnancy. He does respond appropriately and says that when he returns home, he will marry me; however, he is not here now. What is my mother going to say? Her reaction became my greatest concern. Well, to my surprise, my mother was ever so loving and supportive. She told me that I would need to enroll in night school. (Again, back in the day pregnant students could not intermingle with others.)

Oh, how I wished I had continued to say no to having sex, but it was too late now. Even as I write and tell this story, I am embarrassed and ashamed. Even in our sinful lives, some things do work together for the good. God was ordering my steps during these years, preparing me for the road ahead. This experience helped me greatly years later when I was appointed statewide teen parent coordinator. Most teens become pregnant because they get caught up in the moment (looking for love in the wrong places), not because they want to become a mother intentionally.

As I am sure most people do when in certain situations, we pray asking for God to help. I just could never digest the fact that I would not be graduating with my classmates and moving on to college. College was a dream because I wanted to be able to have a meaningful adult life. I had a deep desire to go further than my mom and having a child out of wedlock was not the way. As life would have it, one night, I woke up in excruciating pain which resulted in my having a miscarriage. I was sad but glad. I had not taken any steps to drop out of day school nor began to show any signs of being pregnant, so my friends never knew. I was able to graduate without the whispers of being a parenting teen.

Yes, I went on to college, as planned. The love of my life returned after his tour in Vietnam, and we talked of marriage, but my response at this time was he could not pay for my college education. I found out later that he had fathered two other children and, at some point, gotten married. Oh, how I cried and cried, but I rationalized and said, "So what." He continued to tell me repeatedly that he loved me. I believed him wholeheartedly. (The devil will make a fool out of you even as a sinner.) Now, during this time, I obtained my bachelor's degree and master of education degree. He was still enlisted in the marines and not at home during this period.

Yes, I dated in college while the love of my life was stationed in another state. In fact, during my undergraduate years, I dated a young man for at least two years, but upon his graduation, he returned home and married someone he impregnated. Now, the devil really lays it on and resumes telling me the only way I will get married is to get pregnant. I responded to the devil that this is not the way my marriage will begin. Well, the story doesn't end here regarding the love of my life.

After graduate school, I returned home, and the love of my life is discharged from the marines, and he's home. Of course, we resume our relationship. Like I said, he is the love of my life. He now promises to get a divorce, and of course, I believe him. However, it is at this point that I tell him that if things do not go as they should, I will ask God to take away the feelings I have for him. I got saved, filled with Holy Ghost, and shortly thereafter, left for Chicago because my mom gets sick. The end of this story is told in another chapter.

The spirit of condemnation will come to make you feel depressed and worthless. The devil knows our past. He will pull our file when he thinks you are most vulnerable. A time to watch is holiday seasons, especially Christmas and New Year. There is a heavy spirit during this time period that will attack you greatly. I strongly suggest that if possible, get with some other single sisters and plan an activity together. Have a holiday meal or movie night and talk about fun things, play games, or take a trip. If your church has celebrations, use your talents to decorate or serve on the hospitality committee. (Ask God for something you can do to help others. When I was in high school, I worked as a candy striper in the children's ward of the hospital. Nursing homes would welcome the church to come and sing and read Scriptures to the residents.) There is a myriad of things you can do to occupy your mind during this period. If you are still employed, you can work while the others take vacation. Think about it, the workplace will be quieter, and you can accomplish a lot.

I told you this would be a preachy chapter. James 4:7 states, "Submit yourself therefore to God. Resist the devil, and he will flee from you." You should have received the baptism of the Holy Ghost; therefore, you have no excuse not to be able to stand and fight the devil. Now, you must be willing to want to resist the intrusion of the devil in your mind to think and then act out things that are against God. I don't care if he is the best-looking man you have ever seen; step back. Don't give in to the urge to walk up to him with that smile. When the devil tells you he is interested, you go the other way. Take a detour because there is construction going on, and the devil wants you to fall into one of the potholes he has dug.

By the way, don't let your friends, especially unsaved, set you up. Now, just in case you are one of those computer nerds, God can read, and He knows when you have gone on that singles only website looking for a mate—so what they say they are Christians. God has not changed nor His Word; therefore, He knows how, when, and where to get you hooked up.

God does not and will not change His mind regarding what He said to us because we pout and throw a temper tantrum. God's word is final and settled. Stop letting the spirit of the enemy get you off track of holiness and singleness. Learn to embrace rather than cast it aside. This is a fight, so stop trying to go in another direction. Think about the time you are wasting; this could be causing Mr. Brother Right from getting the signal from God of your location. Cast that imagination down for good. You can make it; it is only a test, so you can have a testimony.

Another way of standing your ground against the devil is to talk out loud. The Word of God is powerful, and as you say each word of Scripture, let it come out of your mouth with force. Speak so you can hear what you are saying to him. Get your favorite Scriptures and recite them to him. Let him know you are victorious because the victor lives in you. You have power to cast down those negative imaginations he sends. You have your war clothes on, twenty-four hours of every day; therefore, you are refusing to allow him the slightest opportunity to enter. Remind him that he was kicked out of heaven to return no more. Testify of the goodness of Jesus. Talk about the love Jesus had for us that He gave His life. Let him know that it was because of Jesus's stripes you were healed from that/those sickness. Call out the danger you may have encountered but God moved on your behalf. Yes, give God all the praise, and the devil has no choice but to flee. He will return, but if it worked the first time, it can/will work again. Keep on praising God no matter what comes your way.

Our biggest mistake in learning to stand against spirits comes when our flesh does not hear the words "I love you" coming in a romantic vein. As I sit and type, we must be firmly established and know that God loves us if we never hear it from another human being. He loved us so much that He sent His Son, Jesus, to die for our sins. The love God has for us is beyond anything I can describe at the present time. His love is what comforts me when I am down. His love healed me when I had cancer. His love is truly a joy-giver when there is nothing but sadness around. It is His love that settles me when I am anxious. His love speaks to me when others put me down. It was His love that calmed me and told me to move forward when others talked about me. It is His love that embraces me with an illumination that no earthly words can describe. It is His love that lifts His standard when the flesh says give up. It is His love that lets me know that this fight is worth it because there is a better life after this life which will be eternal. I am so glad that Jesus loves me. Please know that there are others that love you also. Look around, there are many in your corner.

Before leaving this chapter, let me add another Scripture. "He that hath no rule over his spirit is like a city that is broken down, and without walls" (Proverb 25:28). This speaks to a defenseless city; the enemy can walk in at will. My sister, let the Holy Ghost fortify you daily. Allow the angels whom God has always given watch over you to stay in place. Don't let it be that you give place to the devil. The saying is if you let the devil ride, he will want to drive, so take this earnest heed and hold fast. Rest in the fact that your name is written in the Lambs Book of Life, and there will be no marriage in heaven, so if it be my plight to remain single, I will be the best, most holy, sanctified devil-fighting sister I can be. I will stand my ground of holiness and righteousness all the days of my life. I plan to hear from Jesus say directly to me, well done thy good and faithful servant enter in. Hallelujah and glory to God for the victory over every challenge and obstacle that comes my way. I am a winner.

Ephesians 6:10–11 tells us emphatically, "Finally, my brethren, be strong in the Lord, and in the power of His might. Put on the whole armor of God that ye may be able to stand against the wiles of the devil." This is so direct. We have power to stand against the devil, so we must make sure we keep on the armor. The armor covers all our vital parts—head, heart, lungs, loins, feet—and then, He provided us with a sword to extinguish the fiery darts that come our way. You must use your own personal artillery. Yes, you can stand victorious against the devil with a willing mind and help of God. The helmet of salvation is protection needed for the mind. This is definitely a critical part of armor provided for His saints.

Oooh! Say Can You See?

It would be a great joy if I could hear your initial response upon seeing this title. I am sure the responses would be interesting. Again, I give God the honor, glory, and praise for blessing me to hear His voice and follow. I was told years ago to keep a pen and paper next to my bed so when the Holy Ghost begins to speak to you during the wee hours of the morning, you can jot down what He is telling you. Well, I always have a tablet and several pens available.

Writing this book is causing me to do a painful introspection of myself which I am accepting as therapeutic. I have not always been a self-assured, single, sanctified sister. In fact, there were many times when I wanted to just run and hide under a rock if possible.

On a personal note, I can remember during my employment developing a life skills assessment instrument for pregnant and parenting teenagers for Daniel Memorial. There was nothing available at the time that case managers could use to assist parents in their continued growth and development. Upon my submission of the instrument it was reviewed by experts in the field of obstetrics, pediatrics, nursing, developmental psychology, and social work across the United States. The instrument was subsequently accepted and posted for nationwide usage. (See Daniel Memorial Life Skills for Pregnant and Parenting)

A letter was sent to my employer informing them of the acceptance of the life skills instrument with the inclusion of accolades from the past president of the American Academy of Pediatrics. To my amazement and dismay, I received no acknowledgment of any kind from the agency director or any other ranking department officials. That was a devastating period of my life and it made me wonder and question my self-worth. Today, I can look back and say, it made me a stronger person. I am thrilled to know that I was able to provide something of benefit to social workers nationwide that would aid them in their work with such a special and needed population.

One part of me said you have skills while the other said I am worthless. (There were other negative exploits that had taken place in the workplace.) After much reflection, thought, and continued prayer, I shook myself and let the devil know I was knowledgeable, with great skills and could move forward to advocate on the behalf of children and families; even if management never recognized me. I continued in this employment endeavor until retirement.

The word "can" is defined as to be able to do, make, or accomplish, to have knowledge or skill, to know how, and lastly, to be physically or mentally able. "See" is defined as to notice or become aware of (someone or something) by using your eyes, to have the ability to see, to come to know (discover), to imagine possible, to perceive the meaning or importance of (understand). These two definitions can be interpreted many ways, but I would like for you to read each again, slowly. We must learn to take small steps and pace ourselves. A book begins with the typing of one word. The fact that you have begun to look within is a major step. Scripture says I can do all things through Christ who strengthens me.

"Do" is a small word but has great expectations. Do not put this book down right now unless you are going to get a pen. What do you want to do with your life? What has always been the foremost issue/concern/desire constantly on your heart? What is holding you back from pursuit? Remember this "can do" is all in the will of God, and you will not be operating on your own strength. As you read, I urge you to write in the columns or margins, fold down the corner of a page so you can come back to a certain point. Roll those sleeves, and let's get ready to mark your impact on the Lord's behalf.

Sisters, it might be dark outside, but we have the Light within us. We must take the time to do a deep and introspective look within ourselves. Trust your feelings and know to whom you belong. We cannot allow others to define who we are or what we have. We must begin to recognize the gifts and talents that lie dormant within us and wake them up. Come out of that dark cocoon that we have wrapped ourselves in because of what somebody said or did. The introspection for some of us may go back to our childhood, when many were called ugly, fat, dumb, crazy, and other demeaning names that had a hold on you.

You are more than a conqueror. The devil meant those things said especially during your early years as stumbling blocks to prevent your growth in the Lord. No, they were not right, but you can get over it/them. Be confident in knowing you are more than a conqueror, and you have Jesus Christ and the power of the Holy Ghost living in you. Think about it, you have overcome many trials, tests, and tribulations that some have never recovered from. Let them talk about you. Words do hurt, but we do not have to accept them by allowing them to enter our spirit. Stop rehearsing the past. Bullying has been around for many years. It is incumbent upon us to know ourselves and not look to others to the extent that we live on what they say about us. The devil wants you to see your single life as a stormy sea rather than a tranquil sea whose waters are crystal clear on a beach whose sand is white and glinting when the sun shines upon it. Picture yourself in the most beautiful of places. You are basking in the loving arms of Jesus because of total submission. You are looking through your own eyes that have been washed in the precious blood of Jesus. Know that you are relevant and very precious in the sight of God.

Our lives today should be a sum of past experiences and what we have learned from them. We are not looking through a stained, uncleansed lens. We are seeing our lives from the perspective "we can make it." Because of what I have gone through, I know how to evaluate life's situations as they come upon me. I know lies from truth. I can recognize false alarms. I see the traps and know not to walk in that direction. I know most of my strengths and weaknesses and have the sense not to test God.

Your exterior beauty can only take you so far. But let's face it, beauty is in the eye of the beholder, and this chapter is dedicated to you and how you see yourself. Psalms 146:4 declares loudly in my opinion, "For the Lord taketh pleasure in his people: He will beautify the meek with salvation." Okay, read each word slowly and stop at "He will" beautify. So what are you trying to do? Please do not get me wrong. I am not saying you should look any kind of way. This is a subject that should be discussed in great length among our churches. Before any further dialogue, I would like to add that the Holy Ghost should be a guide in all endeavors of life, but are you allowing Him to lead you or are you watching others.

Sisters, we should dress as nicely as we are financially capable. Now, I must add another caveat, and yes, I am from the "*old* school." Scripture tells us to dress in modest apparel. I know everybody has their own definition of modesty, but I am just saying even during biblical times, they recognized the harlots/ladies of the evening/street walkers or whatever you call them from those following Christ. Let's stop trying to compromise or hold on to the world. Come all the way out even in your dress. Your pastor is not God, and the Scripture is not of any private interpretation. What does the Bible say? "In like manner also, that women adorn themselves in modest apparel, with shamefacedness and sobriety, not with braided hair, or gold, or pearls, or costly array" (1 Timothy 2:9). I am aware we are living in another time period, but there were certainly differences in the clothing of males and females. Our dress is what people see first and then assess us. What kind of assessment is being made of you? Do you have soundness of mind when shopping? Stop trying to push an ungodly issue. Let's be holy and proud in our dress.

Holiness has a standard that is universal. Our pastors do not have the authority to give you permission to go against the Word of God. God is the same yesterday, today, and forevermore. His Word doesn't change. We should have put away wanting to look provocative and sexy for the gazes of men and put on wanting to look "clean." A clean look is a feminine and soft look. There is a look of sanctification that does not denote looking like an old lady. (Please note, there are some elderly, sanctified women that can put younger ones to shame.) Just know, that all fashions are not for everyone; designers are trying to make money by selling clothes.

There are some outfits that "sanctified sisters" should pass by when shopping. Learn how to dress according to your body type. This means some fabrics are not your friends and should never be worn. In selecting outfits, be for real when you look in the mirror and stop listening to the wicked fashion witch whom you believe is your fashion godmother. The Holy Ghost should check you when that length is too short or the print of your underwear is showing it is too tight. Stop letting the salesperson tell you those lies about how good you look, and the Holy Ghost is saying "take it off." Come on now, you know that skirt is way too short and tight; leave it in the store. The way some of us are shaped, we should wear a jacket that is long enough to hide/camouflage those hips. You can still look fashionable. Dress for your size and shape. You might be small/skinny, but jersey knit can grab you in certain areas that are unbecoming of holiness.

One of my personal pet peeves: should the world know you wear knee highs? If you wear them, please make sure your skirt or dress is long enough to prevent public viewing. As a final point, let us all please invest in the proper undergarments. There are stores which can accommodate all sizes. It would be a fantastic idea if church sisters would get together and have someone come in and share what colors, fabric, and outfits are more flattering for the various figures of us sanctified women. Just know that wearing your clothes dragging the ground is not complimentary either. (This is my personal commentary.)

Let holiness become thine way of dressing every day. By the way, don't dress one way for church services and look like a bum going to the grocery store. You are always representing God; therefore, please do not let Him down. We should always want someone to come ask if we are "saved" because we look and act a certain way. Be consistent especially at your place of employment. Others are always watching you. They are just waiting to see if you will mess up, so they can throw it in your face—I thought you were saved? Let us not be a stumbling block to those on the outside. To add another point, what if God has Brother Right for you at the store, and you walk in looking like you've just had a hard nights' sleep; think about that when you decide to make that mad dash out of your door.

Now, our behavior and actions should also exemplify holiness. We should not be loud and boisterous. Having a meek and humble spirit does not mean you allow people to take advantage of you. It is easy to get a point across without hollering and screaming at the top of your voice. Getting an attitude because the waitress brought the wrong item should not cause you to get rude and out of sorts. Have you ever witnessed a sister enter a restaurant and begin to speak loud about the Lord and when her food comes, fusses at the waitress because it isn't what she ordered? Is God pleased? *No!*

I won't say many, but some women don't like or can't stand you because of jealous eyes. It is sad but women will get jealous just observing the manner in which you walk, talk and dress. They assume you operate in a particular mannerism solely based upon their thoughts. I refuse to make any excuses for getting my education while a sinner. I am proud of being a college graduate, homeowner, and recent owner of a Mercedes Benz yet saved and sanctified. There is no shame that I speak standard English. I am not ashamed of the Gospel as I shop for designer suits. I refuse to let the devil and his imps take me there. Please do not get me wrong, I am not referring in any means to putting on a front to impress others.

Let me remind you that it is not what others think or say that count in your spiritual life. What is God saying to you? You need to get out of the mindset of being like sister so and so. The sisters cannot add or subtract one inch from your waist. What does it matter if they don't invite you over for activities and holidays? Learn how to entertain yourself. When you think about it, sometimes, having a bunch of so-called friends is not such a good idea. Why, because oftentimes, group meetings are generally gossiping sessions about some sister/s in the church. There is no growth in this behavior so appreciate not being a part of that in-crowd.

I preached a message years ago entitled "dare to be different." As saints, we are a special and unique people, and sometimes, among our own, we must separate ourselves. Look out among your congregation and see who you can learn from and work with. You should be able to work with all the saints. That's how we actually learn about one another—working with them. Now, as you work with them, you find out they just want to gossip and get into your and others' business. You should first tell them in a polite manner that's not the way of holiness, and if they refuse, separate yourself and walk with the strong.

Just being know, because of our various personalities, some sisters will not become close to one another. This does not mean we don't love you, we are just not compatible. Our ways, thoughts, and mannerism just do not click. Some sisters want to dominate you, and that doesn't work with all sisters. Oil and water do not mix, but each alone is needful. We need one another but should not lean and depend on one another. Some people will seek you out for their own personal reasons and take advantage. (These are not saints but can be found in the church building.) Get with someone that is strong in the Lord. A strong, positive sister will encourage you in the Lord and naturally as well. A strong sister will let you know in love when you have gotten on the wrong track, when your dress is off, or you're headed for destruction. A strong and loving sister will tell you the truth when you ask her a question. A strong sister will not be jealous and talk about you behind your back. A strong sister is not afraid to pray, lead testimony service, work with their hands, and do other things as needed inside or outside the church. A strong sister will provide support without your asking for any assistance.

We all need a strong sister in our corner. I thank God for my strong sister, Mother Audrey, who told me years ago the importance of walking with the strong. She has been a true example in word and deed of being strong in the Lord.

So what does *Oooh! Say Can You See* mean? It means that you need to look at your own self. Stop allowing others to dictate who you are and what you can or should be doing. You are a child of the most high God, and I know beyond the shadow of doubt that He has put something in *you* toward building the kingdom. What He has given you may not win a Nobel prize, but it can certainly bless a child, mother, community, and most importantly, your local church. Are you sitting on the pew waiting for the pastor to assign you a specific job in the church? Please, get off the seat of doing nothing and get busy.

The world has its own standards regarding beauty, and certainly, beauty is in the eye of the beholder. Growing up, I was always the tallest girl in the class, and that was not a positive trait among my generation. As a result of my being ashamed of my height, I tried to stay in the background away from the attention of others. There have been many times that I have had to be in the background. To a certain extent, I am still in the background, and it is not such a bad place. When you think about the background, it provides you a full view of the entire picture from which you can choose where you would like to go.

Thinking back on my teen years and early twenties, I did not have many male suitors. My girlfriends would be talking about their boyfriends, and I had little to contribute to the conversation. That was a lonely period of my life. People said go to college, and there, you will find your husband. Well, I went to both undergraduate and graduate school, however, and never met that person. When I did meet someone while an undergrad, he graduated before me and was out of my life. In graduate school, all the guys I associated with were already married so no prospects. I returned home and began my career, again, I did not meet anyone. I must admit, I was a workaholic. I'm not sure if it was because I didn't have a boyfriend or if it was by choice and my work ethic.

Looking back, I just did not attract anyone. I never had a boyfriend that showered me with gifts and made me feel special, not even the love of my life. Even as a sinner, I had some integrity and self-respect. (Please do not feel sorry for me, I'm okay.) Maybe, it is a good thing. All I can say is this was or is my life, and I accepted it. I now think it was important for me to share this portion of my life in case there are others reading who might be experiencing this same type of male void in their lives today. Yes, at some point, I thought

I was worthless based on not being pretty or attractive according to the world's standards, but having a great mom was my support. As the years have passed, I have developed more confidence in myself. I have done numerous self-examinations and found myself to be a blessed woman of God with abilities that would indeed bring delight to the right man.

Believe it or not, I was once a very quiet person and would not tell you how I felt, but today, it is a different story. I have learned to express my opinion in a respectful manner. Yes, one bad relationship leaves a negative feeling, but I have not put all men in that same box. I am not a set of railroad tracks that you can just ride over at any given time. My confidence is not bossy as some may say. I know what I know and make no excuses. One thing I will not do is put me down so that someone else can shine. Why can't we shine together? I am a complete woman who is waiting for a complete man of God. In the meanwhile, I must do the work of Him that has charged me to teach the Word.

During your quiet time with God, why not ask Him to reveal to you who you are. What are my qualities? What do I do well? With what age groups am I best suited to work with? I am talking beyond cooking in the kitchen. Now, do not get me wrong. There is a need for good cooks, but we are living during a time where souls are at stake, and we need to be soul winners, if that's the direction God is taking you. I am not telling you to go stand on the corner, and evangelize if this is not your calling. There are many other ways souls can be won. You must find your role in kingdom building for Jesus.

Let me insert this little caveat. As sisters of Christ, we all need to get rid of the "she thinks she…" attitude. Why can't we just come together and work even if you are not the leader. Why is it so hard to be of assistance? Come join in making a project successful. *Oooh*, can you see yourself as a weight rather than a helper. Think about this point. The architect only draws the plans for a building; he is not the one that builds. The construction of the building requires many people. You have ability to keep the work moving in your church or organization, what can you do? What are you willing to do? Sisters, it is a *sin* to sit back and watch and complain about someone doing a great work, and you refuse to offer any assistance and can do so. Okay, I must get off this ranting. Nevertheless, as Mother Winters would say, we must move forward.

There is greatness in you that has not been touched. You have willingly allowed the enemy to keep your gifts, talents, and abilities asleep. I implore you as Paul told Timothy in 2 Timothy 1:6, "Wherefore I put thee in remembrance that thou stir up the gift of God, which is in thee by the putting on of my hands." Most of you reading this book have been taught, prophesied, and hands laid upon to do certain works in the church, but you have failed to move. Some of you have become deaf to hearing, and others have no mind to move forward, but in the name of Jesus, I declare and speak that you shall have no rest until you open your eyes, see, and move in the will of God concerning you.

This is chapter 4, and hopefully, you have made some modifications in your life. Do you see a change? Are you pleased with this newness? Everyone expects God to move on our behalf, but we want to stand still. No, it is time for you to wake up out of that deep sleep and see what you can do for the kingdom. We always talk about when we get to heaven; what a time we will have, but guess what, you do not have to wait. God has great and spectacular things for us right here on earth to enjoy. "The blessing of the Lord, it maketh rich, and He addeth no sorrow with it" (Proverbs 10:22). This is so plain; you can be blessed on this earth without sorrow. Some of that sorrow will come from those jealous haters out there. Do not allow them to shake or disturb your enthusiasm and blessings from God. Do not hide what God has done for you. Tell of His goodness among the congregation of the righteous. At one point of my life, I did not tell what God was doing for me because I was afraid of the people and what they were saying, but I came to myself. God has done these great and mighty things for me. He has blessed me to afford a luxury car, another fur coat, and ability to travel near and far. Why should I hold my peace? Declare God's goodness on the mountaintop.

Yes, I deserve and am worthy of everything God has given to me. I have walked worthy, suffered, and endured. Glory to God for His love toward us. I am ready to preach now, but Psalm 84:11, "For the Lord God is a sun and shield: the Lord will give grace and glory: no good thing will He withhold from them that walk uprightly." Let the people talk. The more they talk, and you endure, the more God will bless. Let the church say, "Amen!"

After you have done the will of God, you can see yourself clearly. Once you get in the right mode of God, you will be able to see and appreciate the abundance God has bestowed upon you. The haze will be lifted, and the blue skies and billowy white clouds will gently sail by you. You will be lifted into a place of peace that you have never experienced or knew existed. Come out! Come out and let God show you just how beautiful, precious, and loving you are to Him. Let Him reveal the manifold blessings in store for you when really see *you*! Open your eyes, it is but for the asking. It is me, oh, Lord, standing in Your need.

Now, once God reveals to you your work, don't get afraid or hesitate. There will be those that will speak negative, but you stand inside the bubble of God. Stay securely nestled in the hollow of His arms. Every project may not be the greatest of success but continue and don't give up. Don't worry if you get no help; remember, God told you what to do and not the crowd. You will learn how to be persistent and how to persevere when things become difficult. In your quest to fulfill God's plan in your life, know that it is you that must do the work. Ask yourself, how far are you willing to go? How hard will you work to reach the goal He has established for you? Are you a quitter because you must go alone when others promised to help? What will you do when you must spend your own money and might put you in a pinch? God said He would never leave you nor forsake you; will you leave the job unfinished?

Oh, say can you see yourself in the presence of Jesus? Picture yourself hearing Him say, "Well done, my good and faithful servant. You kept the faith and did not let the fact of being single prevent you from fulfilling your assignment." There is a benefit package, and God is generous to us. Think on Psalm 1:3: "And he shall be like a tree planted by the rivers of water, that bringeth forth his fruit in his season; his leaf also shall not wither; and whatsoever he doeth shall prosper." Accept the Word of God, and it will be a blessing to you.

Lose the Humpty-Dumpty Syndrome

Many of you know the story of Humpty Dumpty sitting on the wall, falling, and no one being able to put him back together. Well, this is another epiphany given to me by the Holy Spirit to help my single sisters. I would like to look at this syndrome from several vantage points—not accepting/acknowledging your true self (burying weaknesses; paying more attention to influences of others; not taking heed to warnings; and knowing if you are on sure foundation). Just keeping it real, it is time to let go and let God.

Humpty was an un-boiled egg, and everyone knows that great care should be taken when placing an egg on just any type of surface. If you are truly a saint of God, then you cannot be in just any type of church. Saints are precious commodity and should not be handled any kind of way. In fact, eggs are perishable and must be handled with great care. We must be in the church that God has told us to attend/join because He will have a leader who will know how to nurture you. Your leader will know where you should be especially as it relates to the body of Christ. They will know how and what to do to get you to that place if you are willing and obedient.

You are only one individual and cannot conquer/save the world alone. You must be fully aware of your strengths and weakness and face them. Thinking you can accomplish something is totally different than having the ability to carry it to fruition. I might think I can climb the highest mountain but can't walk two Chicago blocks. Get real. On the other hand, you must recognize your frailties and acknowledge them also. If you are afraid to fly, you will not be traveling overseas or an island. If you cannot speak before more than three people at a time, then the mission field is not for you. Know your place and where you fit. If you are under capable and wise church leadership, have a talk with your pastor regarding some of the things you think you might be capable of performing or would like to do. He will let you know if it is something you should pursue and ready to handle. Don't get upset if he tells you to wait. Continue to work on improving yourself in that area.

Now, Humpty was sitting on a ledge, and the people could see him very well. You might be someone with many talents and is frequently called upon by the pastors and others to do a myriad of things because of your talents, but beware. Don't bite off more than you can chew. You want to perform to the best of your ability. Also, take care not to get overconfident. There are others that can perform equally if not better than you. Don't let the accolades of people cause you to move around so much that you lose your balance.

Yes, people are looking up to you for a variety of reasons, but are you fulfilling what God wants? Are you just there to please the people? If what you are doing is not prosperous or edifying to the body of Christ, you come down on your own. Should this be a work for God, give Him the glory and honor for allowing you to work in His stead, because without Him, you could not do anything. Lift up Jesus in all that you say and do. God give the increase. Yes, you can boast, but make sure it is in the Lord.

It is a shame to say this but, caution must be taken that you do not allow people to prey upon you. Take heed, do not listen to those calling you out, daring you to jump when they want you to do so. Why should you jump into something without the approval from God? Why would you take on more than you can handle? Do not let people use or take advantage of you. There are those who want you to always give to them but they seldom if ever extend a giving hand. This includes loaning money that takes them too long to repay. Watch that person that slides next to you and says, Sister you should give me that suit you are wearing. Yes, stay humble but do not become a floor mat for others. Enjoy the blessings God has bestowed upon you. Many do not know your story or from where God has brought you.

There comes a time in each of our lives that we must "take control." Why are you allowing others to lead and guide you in a direction that you are uncomfortable and know isn't you? Sometimes, we can admire people so that we take on their character and begin acting and talking like them. Be yourself! It takes too much effort from you to try and emulate another person. Take a good look within and be proud of you. You may not have reached that point you desire, but with perseverance, you will make it. Keep climbing until you reach your top. Identical twins do not have the same fingerprint, so there is only one *you*! Recognize who you are in God and work on you with all your might.

Second Timothy 2:19 states, "Nevertheless the foundation of God standeth sure, having this seal. The Lord knoweth them that are His. And let everyone that nameth the name of Christ depart from iniquity." God's foundation will never crumple or detonate ever; therefore, if we follow Him, we can be sure not to fall.

As we continue to look at this egg syndrome, sometimes, we forget and put it on the wrong surface, and the next thing you realize, it has fallen and shattered into many pieces. You now have a real mess to clean up. Think about your life. Sometimes, we make mistakes— wrong decisions—and our lives become shattered. Now, we can look at this as both good and bad. It was bad that we fell, yes, for whatever reason we yielded to the word from the enemy. We could have just given in because we were tired of waiting on God to move in the time span we thought was allowable for us. Mistakes should show us ourselves if we would only take the time to really look inward.

"For all have sinned and come short of the glory of God" (Romans 3:23). If you look at the words "have sinned," it does not read "sinning." So you should not permit yourself to continue being in a sinful state. Acknowledge that you failed to attend church when you could have but chose to stay home; decided to use your tithes for something personal; allowed the root of bitterness to take over because in your eyes, Sister So and So seemed to be the pastor's favorite; and other various things you don't like in the church. Well, you are all broken up, so what are you going to do with your life? Do you want to stay a mess? Do you want to continue walking around all marred? Flesh will have you go to your "friend" who is also broken.

Now, I ask, how can someone who is broken provide you with instructions? Certainly, the blind cannot lead the blind. This is another trick of the devil. The enemy will bring someone to befriend you during your most gullible period of despair. He wants to make you weak as water and loss sight of your spiritual goals. My momma often quoted, birds of a feather flock together. Yes, looking at your current situation there appears to be no way out. Because of your surroundings the mind says just go ahead and blend in, but your spirit is saying no to the blend. Your spirit is very much aware that you can do better. It is my hope that reading this book will be the beginning of your wanting to improve the status of your life. Things get much better when Christ is on your side.

One of the prime symptoms of this chapter is how we, as women, are impacted by the thoughts of others. Yes, we must and should be careful when sharing our past lives. It was only after prayer that I have elected to share such personal and private information about my life. Yes, confession is good for the soul, but think about your audience when making confessions, as well as the purpose for the said confession.

Unlike Humpty Dumpty, I am no longer a frail, fragile and helpless/insecure, single, sanctified woman. I am bold and powerful in the Lord. It is sad to say, but some people will remember a sister's past until she dies rather than the life she lived in Christ. Folks will look down upon individuals without any regard or remembrance of the sins they were actively involved in as a sinner. Everyone should remember that we sinned against God, and He sent His Son to die on the cross for our sins. When we repent, our sins were cast in the sea of forgetfulness, so why do people want to remember them?

My sisters, be mindful and prayerful to whom you share portions of your past life. If your church has a testimony service, the purpose is to share with the saints the spiritual blessings God has performed on your behalf. It is not necessary to tell all the events of your sinful life. What is the purpose? Are you prepared for the aftershock both spoken and unspoken? Foremost, what is your motive for sharing? Some testimonies of your deliverance are for a special population at a time when God has put you in a place to share for His glory. Be mindful also that some saints have a severe case of selective amnesia regarding when they were sinners. Some people would love to keep you on that wall, so you will fall and shatter beyond recognition with no hope of repair. They know that once you become whole, your sanctification will show them up. It is sad, but there are those you must leave behind.

Shake yourself and acknowledge the error of your ways and repent. Stop trying to repair yourself. Your bandages, gorilla glue, duct tape, or any other adhesive remedies are not going to work. It is a must that you go down to the potter's house: "And the vessel that he made of clay was marred in the hand of the potter, so he made it again another vessel, as seemed good to the potter to make it." (Jeremiah 18:4). God can fix you in such a way that you will be surprised when you look in the mirror. He will renew your mind and refill you with the Holy Ghost, thereby putting your name back into the Book of Life. Stop thinking you can handle it and let God do it. Take the limits off God and learn to rest in Him. There comes a time in our lives that we must realize we cannot fix ourselves. Isaiah 48:10 states, "Behold, I have refined thee, but not with silver; I have chosen thee in the furnace of affliction." Your affliction might come in a variety of ways; but it can be overcome. God's afflictions come to show us where we are in Him. You can make it.

Recognize, acknowledge, and accept who you are in Christ. You can only do what He allows you to do. Stay in the ship and realm of God. Abide in the ship—our ark of safety—which is in the arms of Jesus. Let Jesus lead, guide, direct, and order your steps. We do not know the way except we be led by the Spirit of God. Follow the leader, and you won't fall. We are precious to Jesus, and if we follow Him, it will prevent us from falling and getting those scraps, bumps, and bruises.

Should you fall and get all cracked up, just know you do not have to stay in a cracked-up and broken state. God is a forgiving God and knows all our weaknesses and impending failures. He knew we were going to fail when we thought we were strong and could hold on and go through. He knows our mind. So you failed and cried and cried and cried, but now, it is time to get up. You might have gone out and married that man because he said he was saved, but after the "I-dos" and "I-wills," he changed. The wolf will put on sheep's clothing just to get a good sistah out of the church. But God is not willing that any should perish. Guess what, that is why He sent His son, Jesus, to be our reconciliation. We can come back, submit ourselves to Him, and He will put us back together for His use.

God is a master builder, and sometimes, the new, improved, and renovated is much better than the original. Don't be ashamed to return to God. He is no longer ashamed of you. In fact, come on back and share your testimony to the others in hopes they will listen and not fall into the same trap. Expose the devil for the liar he is and describe the tricks he used to get you out of Christ. Let the world know you are back to fight the good fight of faith. Broken in Christ does not mean destroyed. God does put the pieces back together for His glory, honor, and praise.

6

What's in Your Cup?

Well, well, well, are you sitting down? Let me try to paint a colorful picture for you. As you sit at your table with your favorite cup, what are you about to pour into it? Now, I put my cream and sugar in my cup before pouring in the hot coffee. Doing it this way seems to allow the coffee to interact with the other substances quicker and making it easier to dissolve. What is your favorite morning beverage?

We control how much or how little we want in our cups. There are times when we only want a small amount, and other times, we seem to have the cup overflowing with liquid, thus making a mess that we must clean up. If the liquid is extra hot, we have sometimes dropped the cup and its contents on the floor. What's most important is that if nothing is poured into the cup, you will have nothing to drink.

The events of our lives are the contents of our cup. We generally are aware of most events that we expect to happen in our lives; however, there are those days when the unexpected happens, and this is when we begin to wonder, *What in the world is going on?* In some situations, we can control what is placed in our cup, but when we come to God, we are in His will.

"I will take the cup of salvation and call upon the name of the Lord" (Psalms 116:13). The psalmist who wrote this was aware of the power, blessings, and deliverances of God. He had a relationship with Him. Now, we are His daughters. Living in the dispensation of grace and truth, there are certain things which have been made available to us. Upon our accepting Jesus as our Savior, our cup contains the fruits of the Spirit—love, joy, peace, longsuffering, gentleness, goodness, faith, meekness, and temperance. I will not describe the fruit, but they each have a unique role in our sanctified life, and it is imperative that we learn how to activate each when necessary. Love is the generator of them all. Love will be one that is constantly used, because no matter what, who, or how the situation or circumstance is looking in that cup, you must be accepting. If by accident, you drop the cup (fail the test) and break it into pieces, it is coming back around. Our cup comes in various sizes and shapes; however, it is capable to handle *all* temperatures from freezing to boiling hot.

Let's go directly to sickness, as something that will certainly come upon you as we grow older. We were made of the dust, and we shall certainly return. Our bodies are fearfully and wonderfully made, but they do break down. Maybe, for some of you reading this, you have always been sickly, therefore, think of the encouragement you can provide to others. You know God delivers.

From my perspective, when sickness comes upon us, there is a willingness/melting/embracing that must take place in the mind. In short order, we must accept the situation rather than trying to pray it away (yes, we should and must pray). I do not mean giving up or surrendering to the sickness to take you out—die—but, rather, accepting what has befallen you at this point in your life. Yes, the illness may be life threatening, but remember, our life is in God's hands. It is God Almighty who has the final say regarding your living or dying. It is during these times that we need the consolation and comfort that only God can provide to and for us. It is at this point your trust and dependency should deepen upon the Lord. God knows the path we must take and will never leave us, especially during those difficult times.

In 2015, I was diagnosed with uterine cancer. I had not been having female problems and maintained regular checkups. When I should have been experiencing menopause and wasn't, my gynecologist teased me that I should be careful because of the possibility of me becoming pregnant. (At this point, I am sixty-two, and I know there will be no more immaculate conceptions.) Well, to make a long story short, she decided to conduct another test, and this one revealed cancer. Yes, I was proclaiming to be cancer free, but I was not so fortunate. The gynecologist gave me the grim news, but my immediate response was, "I'm going to be all right." She was looking so sad that I had to cheer her up before leaving the office.

She referred me to a wonderful and gentle oncologist who performed surgery followed by chemo treatments. (I had never been in the hospital before, so this was all new to me.) The chemo treatments resulted in my losing my hair. Praise the Lord for wigs. Oh, yes, the devil tried to work on my mind, but I kept the faith. I continued to attend regular church services on Tuesdays, Thursdays, and Sundays with very few absences except when I was too tired. At this point, I pause to give special thanks to my big sisters (Mother Audrey Hicks and Evangelist Henri Winters) for being present at each treatment. I give special accolades to Mother Hicks for her impeccable nursing attributes and attending to my every need without hesitation after my surgery. Mother Hicks will make you want to stay in bed because of her constant attentiveness.

The treatments included blood test and physical examinations that must take place at three– then six-month intervals, and finally, yearly. The enemy wars continue with my mind when it's time to take another blood test or physical exam because he wants me to think the cancer is not gone. I must talk to myself that I am healed. As I expose more of myself writing this book, I also acknowledged that I was ashamed when I received the diagnosis. My thought was, *God, why me? I've been faithful, and You allowed this to happen to me.* Well, I received no revelation but shook myself and went on to follow the doctors' orders. I did not complain or share this with friends or as a testimony. I have finally come to the point of being able to share this as a testimony. Believe it or not, I have yet to share this with one of my close friends. One day, I may, but I know she's going to ask too many questions as to why I did not. I did not want to burden her with my medical issues as she had lost another friend during my time of treatment.

We should know our family history, and as much as lies within us, do those things that will keep our bodies healthy. Yes, we should get annual physical examinations. As we get older, our bodies change, so we will need to modify our diets. I am the last to push exercise, but know, sitting in the chair or sofa all day is not healthy.

Oh, yes, things will come upon you without warning, but most times, we set the stage based on our actions, behaviors, and temperament. One thing saints should not do is "get common" with God. What do I mean? Because we may have been very faithful and dutiful in service to God during a certain period of our lives, does not mean we can now relax and sit on our laurels or retire from working for the Lord. Oh God knows me, so I don't really have to be as dutiful. I might be in my sixties, but I am yet attending every service possible, day and night. I continue to support church projects regardless if I am spearheading it or not. I don't want to be one of those mothers sitting in the corner talking about what I use to do and still able bodied enough to continue. We must endeavor to be fervent in the spirit. If we think about it, God is older than all of us, and He continues to bless us every day and knows our abilities. We should maintain our diligence and faithfulness in attending services. We should not get to the place where we get slack and think God is going to excuse us based on our age and past endeavors. We must work while we have the strength, mind, and ability to perform. The bible clearly reads that we should maintain good works.

I mentioned earlier about temperature, well, most cups are made to handle high heat. We also must know that we will sometimes be put in the fire of afflictions. These afflictions may not be physical in nature but psychological and spiritual. The devil uses all kinds of tactics against us so that we will give up on God. When the devil notices you cannot handle a single incident, he will increase the forces that come against you as if shooting a machine gun. The things around you will seem as if everything is closing in on you. It is at this point that you check and ensure you are wearing all of your armor, especially the helmet of salvation.

Think about Jeremiah. He was lowered into a hole in the ground because he spoke the words of God. We can say he got hot and declared he would no longer speak on God's behalf, *but* he could not hold his peace. Why? He had committed/dedicated himself to the work of the Lord. Jesus did not quit when things got hot and heavy for Him prior to being led to Calvary. Jesus was beaten in a manner that no human could have withstood solely to bring us back to His Father.

Think about this; when you go out to eat, you are not totally aware of all the ingredients in your beverages and entrée. I'd like to share, briefly, another incident that happened in my life. There was a brother in the church that gave me a plastic bag one day. When I looked in the bag, it contained an empty ring box. *What is the meaning of this?* I asked myself. *How should I address this? Is this something I should be happy about?* Well, I was not impressed, and the more I thought, I became angry. I haven't the slightest idea why he would assume such a gesture would make me happy in the least bit. A marriage had recently taken place at the church, but I certainly made no comments to him about my wanting to marry—least of all him. He was a nice brother who would do minor things for me, but I was not sending out any kind of message. This was puzzling, and I went to both saved and unsaved men to ask their opinion of this, and they could not provide any reasonable explanation. Well, I gave the wrinkled bag and its non-impressive contents back to the brother.

Sisters, examine the substance in your cup and don't be so anxious to accepting anything. Common sense should click in. Don't be so gullible. Know whose you are, always. Royalty only accepts royalty. Do not allow yourself to go from drinking from a golden cup to a paper cup because your flesh is excited. God forbid, calm down and be patient.

The War Is On... How Will You Come Out?

What is the war? It is the battle with the devil with your mind and flesh. Now, in case you were not aware, or captured what I have revealed I have not been saved all my life. I accepted Christ at the age of twenty-eight years old. My ultimate coming to Christ, of course, was because I heard the word and took heed. Let me share a portion of my story. Yes, repeating, I began dating, yes, a tall, dark, and handsome man the summer of my impending senior year of high school. My girlfriend introduced him to me as he was a good friend of her boyfriend. He was two years older than me and, of course, had an automobile. At the time, I had no idea he had other girls on the string, as they said back in the day.

During my senior year he joined the Marines and went off to war. I diligently sent him at least one letter a week, drenched in my perfume. (I wanted him to recognize my letters.) Anyway, to make a long, sad story short, when he came home, we resumed dating. I graduated high school and college while he continued serving our country. After college, I returned home and so did he. However, to my lack of knowledge, he was also seeing someone else, and she got pregnant. He married after a period of time and, of course, I did not know.

Now, as a sinner, I really didn't care because I was in love, and he never really told me himself that he was married. I continued to see him thinking I was the one and could change him from his ways, but it did not work. Now, my female friends told me that all men have dogs in them, and I would have to submit to this way of thinking. Well, I disagreed with this notion wholeheartedly. As I recall, I never allowed my personal life to interfere with my employment and community involvements. I was the director of a community action council and had memberships in other organizations. No, I was not about to sit at home and feel sorry for myself even then. I was attending and actively involved in my church (not saved). Also included in my itinerary of life was a sudden desire to run for councilwoman. I decided to run so that I could be a part of the process to help my fellow brothers and sisters locally and, eventually, become the first female African-American president of the United States. (Well, I did have some lofty dreams.) In my pursuit to win this office, I visited Fifth Street Church of God of West Palm Beach, Florida, to ask members for their vote on election day. They invited me to an upcoming revival. Being a woman of my word, I went to the revival, and guess what? I accepted Jesus as my Savior and was baptized with the Holy Ghost and spoke in tongues.

God's ways are truly not our ways, and He knows what is best for us. I had no understanding of what really happened to me that night. I recall holding my mouth as the Holy Ghost moved upon me. A mother kept telling me to be glad, and I just smiled until, finally, I gave up completely, and the tongues began to speak. This was a joy I never experienced before. No, I did not praise God in my other church, this was for the old folks, but I found out differently that night. By the way, I did not win the election but received something that I have been able to cherish for over forty years with no regrets. The best event to happen in my life was the gift of salvation. It was at this point that my life really began.

Well, salvation was a new adventure in my life, and I was not in a holiness church. Praise the Lord, the Holy Ghost is a leader, guide, and teacher. Now, I knew the love of my life was messing around on me but felt because I loved him, and he said I loved me too, things would get better. Yes, I was a silly, foolish and naïve woman. Some say they are looking for love, but I will just say it is the closeness and intimacy that many seek. Let me just add, when your friends and society all say the way to marriage is via sexual intimacy, what other path should you be expected to follow? I was still in a sexual relationship with him despite the fact that he was married. Remember he never told me directly, so I just hung in there. But one day, he came to my house (yes, I had my own home back then) and wanted to hug, but the Holy Ghost immediately let me know I could not remain in that relationship. In fact, the Holy Ghost told me directly that I could not continue to ask for forgiveness and remain committing the same sin. Yes, my conscious was telling me this is wrong. (Sisters, we know that fornication and adultery is wrong on all avenues. There is no way we can compromise our thinking that it isn't wrong. Even when the doctor tells you you, need to engage in sex.)

During another visit, as he attempted to hug and kiss me, I told him this relationship could not continue. I ran and hid behind my bedroom door until he left. Even as I recount my past life event of forty years ago, I am deeply repentant and sorrowful in sharing. The enemy wants me to be self-conscious and not share in fear of what those readers who know me will think. Again, the warfare continues as I mentioned earlier, but we are overcome by our testimony. That was a victorious day but not the end of the story. I had no more relations with him, but yes, I still had strong feelings for him.

Shortly, thereafter, I left West Palm Beach and came to Chicago because my mom was ill. No, my affections for him did not leave despite the distance. My brother died about one year later, and I returned home to assist with funeral arrangements and be with other siblings. Yes, I called him upon my return and informed him of my brother's death. (He is no longer married.) I don't recall if it happened during or after the call, but I felt something come out of me. I no longer had the "love" affection for him as before. Yes, I had prayed and asked God to remove it, and God answered my prayer. Still being young in the Lord, I did not comprehend some spiritual things, but I knew God had done something for me when he walked into the house.

Being a longtime friend, the love of my life arrived at my sister's home to extend his condolences. Yes, he was still looking good and the flesh missed him. There was no intimate hugging and kissing when he arrived. Now, the devil is an accuser of the brethren and knows your past, therefore he began to take my mind back to those romantic times. The devil begins to say you are miles away from Chicago and no one will know if you resume the relationship. I admit that for a fleeting moment of time I thought of the possibility of getting back with the love of my life. Guess what? I no longer had that feeling of love for him, hallelujah. I really came totally to myself and made a decision of decisions that very day by submitting to the Holy Ghost. We went on to discuss family members and as a result the conversation shifted.

I do not remember his exact words, but he expressed great love and affection for me. He began to say words with great emotion that I had always wanted to hear from his lips to my ears, but guess what, they were too late. He talked about coming to Chicago, but I commented he could not stay with me as I was still saved. He went on to talk about wanting to be with me and telling me all the things I desired him to say years earlier, but his words fell on dry soil. Keeping it real and being transparent, he was still physically good looking and had an excellent job. I had not seen anyone in the church here in Chicago I was remotely interested or attached to. Yes, having a sound mind during time of adversity is important. I remained steadfast and unmovable. It was at that point, I felt the Spirit of God move upon me and in lightning speed, and I felt the very desire for him to leave. It was a refreshing feeling. I was polite but not giddy.

The Holy Ghost will lift up a standard if you want to be kept. This was a major battle for me and thank God for being victorious. Some of you might think I should have encouraged him to come to Chicago; he might have gotten saved because maybe that was my husband. The devil is a liar. I was not even directed by the Holy Ghost to witness in words to him; he was a witness of my life. The end of this story is, this friend whose name was Kenneth died some years later of a drug overdose I am told, and his body was found days later. One of his sisters told me years later that he would often talk about me and was sorry that our relationship ended as it did. I have no regrets. I ran for my life, and I am glad about it. Oh, the joys of being with Jesus.

Spirit is willing, but Flesh is weak. Those flashbacks are going to happen without warning, but we must know how to cast them down. There was a period when the devil would bring dreams to me of the love of my life. Years after his death, I began to have dreams of this love of my life and would wonder because my mind was not on him at all. He was dead. My mind was certainly not on him at any time. I would rebuke the devil in my dreams and thank God when I woke up. Yes, it was a fight, but I am a winner.

Yes, I admit to being one that romanticizes and expecting a happy ending or, better yet, waiting for a knight in shining armor to come sweep me away. But I also believe in being real with myself. I am not going to settle for less than the best. My sisters, just be real with yourself. There is a lot of talk regarding waiting for your Boaz, but if you really read the story, you would see that Ruth was a worker. She was not idle. She knew her mother-in-law did not have other sons, but she loved Naomi. Ruth did as instructed by Naomi.

What qualities do you have? Are you willing to be submissive? Ruth worked hard in the field to provide for her mother-in-law. Are you working now to provide for yourself or just waiting for someone to provide all your necessities? Do you have a bank account, or do you spend all your money on hair weave, clothes, etc.? Do you know how to cook a complete and balanced meal? Do you know how to budget your finances? Do you know how to keep a clean environment? Do you know how to wash clothes properly? Do you know how to be quiet? Are you selfish? Are you jealous? Are you willing to share? These are just a few of the questions you must not only ask yourself but also answer them honestly. What are you bringing to the table? No sane, intelligent, holy man of God is looking for a "needy" sister.

At this point, I would strongly suggest if your purpose for a husband is only to be "taken care of," you need to go search yourself. Marriage is a two-way street; you are responsible for some things also and, more than your body.

Yes, there is a war going on in our mind. As I think on many situations people encounter and constantly discuss. It all goes back to the mind. There is a lot going on in the mind, but who is controlling your thoughts? Saints should not surrender their minds to the devil. There are so many Scriptures that tell us what to do to combat this onslaught from the devil. If we keep our minds stayed on Him, yes, He will keep us in perfect peace, but sometimes, we just can't/don't. We begin to reflect on incidents of the past and get caught up. The thoughts of wishing we had not done this or that, or just why did I say that? There must be a willingness to manage our thoughts.

For those of you that were sexually abused, you question yourselves constantly. What did I do to deserve such treatment? Why was I not believed? Know, sometimes, there are no answers to many questions regarding why certain things occurred in our lives. Sin is the root cause of many things that have befallen us, and yes, God was there all the time. Remember, Jesus came and bore all these on the cross for us. He knew we could not carry such enormous burdens. He gave instructions for us to cast our cares upon Him because He cares for us. Once we cast those cares and set our affections above, the hurt, pain, and distress we suffered over the years will begin to go away. You have a scar as a reminder of the hurt and pain but know it has been cast into the sea of forgetfulness to be remembered no more. We will no longer cry at night because of thoughts that come to cause sleepless nights. We have sweet sleep because of our trust and hope in Christ. We are winners!

You might ask me how I behaved in the workplace. Of course, there were men, but I carried myself in such a lady-like and sanctified manner that it was rare for any of the men to approach me in a negative or inappropriate manner. I recall one of my coworkers offering to introduce me to one of his friends because he said I needed a husband. In fact, he provided me with a list of men from which I could choose. Of course, I declined his offer. I developed an invisible Holy Ghost shield that emitted a shock which kept men away. I do not consider myself attractive, but I also did not place myself in positions that would be considered a "come on." I was not the giddy, childish woman that sought the praise of men. Being foolish in your youth isn't pretty, and it certainly doesn't look good on you when you get old. Learn from your mistakes; stop repeating the same behavior, expecting a different outcome.

I am reminded of another situation that happened to me. While in a downtown Walgreens one afternoon, as fate would have it, a guy walked up to me and asked if I was Frances Elbert. I replied yes. He remembered me from our being in eighth grade together, and he was the first boy I ever kissed. (So, I guess he was my first boyfriend). Of course, I did not recognize him until he told me his name. We exchanged phone numbers. Well, I said to myself, "This is it. If he calls, I am certainly going to go out because it has been a long time since I have been in the company of a man on a date."

Yes, he called, and we talked at great length from eighth grade to now—over twenty plus years. He's divorced, and I should have been the mother of his children. All the right things I thought I wanted to hear. Well, I did tell him I was saved and sanctified, living for the Lord. During that time, I had planned a dinner at my home because I had gotten in contact with two other classmates from eighth grade. Guess what, he did not attend the planned dinner nor did he ever call me again. This was a victory, and God did not even allow me to be tested. God knows better than we, actually how much we can bear.

There have been other wars that I have experienced, and they were against my mind. I learned how not to entertain those thoughts but rather to rebuke the devil at that point in time. We must learn how to busy ourselves with the works of the Lord. If we tire the physical body, we can eliminate some pressures, but within, we must ultimately want to stay with God. The warfare will remain until we die, but we can keep the devil at a distance. Isaiah 26:3 states, "Thou wilt keep him in perfect peace, whose mind is stayed on Thee: because he trusted in Thee." This lets us know for certain that if we keep our minds on the one who saved us, the one who brought us out of a world of sin can certainly keep us now no matter what we are encountering. He will never leave us. What is the worry? We are more than conquerors, and victory is always our goal.

I cannot close this chapter without discussing prophecies. Receipt of a prophecy is very touchy and serious. First, you must know the person speaking is truly saved, sanctified, filled with the Holy Ghost, and being led by God. There are some not led by God but, want you to think they are blessed with the gift of prophesy. Words are powerful, and we must be extremely careful with words from others entering our minds. Does this person exhibit the fruit in the area of prophesy, meaning, does what they report God has told them come to pass?

Now, if they bear the fruit, your only responsibility is to wait. You cannot make this come to pass. In fact based on your behavior, you might prolong its coming into fruition. God knows when, where, how, and who He will use to bring things into existence. This could be a test of your faith. Are you going to stop being faithful in doing God's work? A prophesy may not come to pass for some years. What will you do in the interim? Will your actions toward God change if it does not come when or, more importantly, how you think? Just firmly plant in your mind Isaiah 55:8: "For my thoughts are not your thoughts, neither are your ways my ways, saith the Lord." This is a perfect example that we do not think like God; therefore, we should not be wasting precious time trying to figure how He is going to bring a change in your life. As they say in the world, you do you and let God take care of His business because He does not need our help. God does not need any of our intervention techniques.

There is a war going on, but you are not always in fight mode. The enemy must retreat if you are casting down those imaginations by the power of the Holy Ghost. Jesus knew we would have those times when we would be troubled but John 14:27 states, "Peace I leave with you, my peace I give unto you: not as the world giveth, give I unto you. Let not your hearts be troubled, neither let it be afraid." Jesus spoke these words to His disciples when informing them of His impending death. He was preparing them for what's ahead, and there was no need to be afraid. Likewise, when the Holy

Ghost was sent to Earth to empower those that want to live for Jesus, one of the fruits of the Spirit that is included is "peace."

Peace is defined as being in a state of tranquility or quiet and freedom from disquieting or oppressive thoughts or emotions. "And the very God of peace sanctify you wholly; and I pray God your whole spirit and soul and body be preserved blameless unto the coming of our Lord Jesus Christ" (1 Thessalonians 5:23). So take a deep breath and focus on living for Jesus and being ready to be caught up with Him should He come before death. You know to make it simple. Let us all just keep first things first and seeking first the kingdom of God and His righteousness and all other things shall be added. Not one of our thoughts can cause Jesus into moving before the designated time set for us. Just know you are a winner.

The war is on during those spring and summer months when weddings are taking place seemingly all around you. There are also those times when you are walking through the malls, and you see pregnant moms as well as precious babies being pushed in the carriers. It is a beautiful sight to behold. It might be that special time of the month when your hormones are at its peak, and you feel a certain way. Okay, the enemy will, for certain, want you to go into having a full-blown pity party. He will begin the conversation that you are all alone Immediately interrupt him. You are never alone. The Holy Ghost is with you all the time. I will not give in to having a pity party now or ever. I will and shall press my way through this. Get your focus on the purpose for shopping today and what additional tasks are before you. Keep the focus and do not change the script of course.

Single *With* Children

This chapter came as an afterthought, but I feel it is very important. Some of you may be single parents because your spouse has died (widowed), divorced, or had children out of wedlock prior to becoming saved. God knows your situation and circumstances better than you. You may, at times, regret having children, but they are a blessing. There are many women who wish and pray daily for the ability to have a child but cannot. Your primary concern should be striving to be the best parent with the help of God. I have not given birth to any children, but I strongly believe with my many years of experience in this arena that I can provide some beneficial knowledge that may be of some assistance to you in your being single with children.

Prioritize your life. Yes, you have children; however, Jesus must be first. Jesus must be first and foremost in your life, and you will remain faithful and dedicated to Him. It is Jesus who will be the one to help you in providing for your child/children. Jesus does not accept second place. Jesus is the one you must depend upon in the midnight hours when they get sick, begin acting up (especially teen years), and when you are just at your wits' end. There may be times when you may have to disappoint your child/children because of spiritual obligation but explain this to them. Maintain time to spend with the Lord in prayer and let the children see you praying and studying God's Word. Please, please, please, do not constantly say to the children because of their every negative behavior, it is of the devil, and they are going to hell.

Saints tend to blame the devil for everything when we know that all mankind was born into sin. There is a significant difference when the devil gets involves. So take a deep breath. Our children should experience the loving kindness that God has given to His saints as they grow up within your sanctified walls. They should be able to tell others without hesitancy that their mother lived a holy life. So keep Jesus first and the children next. Pray and seek the Lord in how to raise your child/children, and He will guide you. When God directs you in a path regarding your child, please take heed; He knows what's best for them.

Pray with your children before they leave home in the morning, and as they get older, have them to pray. Instill in them that God wants to hear from them and that God is dependable and available any hour of the day or night. Let them know that He sees all; therefore, they can go to Him about any situation. Live so that your children see the light of Jesus in your life.

The first and foremost step of a single parent is accepting the fact that you are not forgotten or thrown under the bus no matter why you are now the sole caretaker in raising your child/children. It was not in your planning to raise your child/children alone; however, it is what it is, so let's move forward in a positive manner. You do not know what the future holds, so just take a deep breath and move on. God has entrusted you with this responsibility, and you must perform to the highest potential. You have the job of teaching and, more importantly, living a life that those children will emulate. Take inventory of what you are doing to ensure you are raising healthy and productive citizens. Are you taking them to Sunday school, so they can learn and be actively exposed to the Bible principles? Are you allowing them to actively participate in church-sponsored events? (This is a time where you can get some relief/rest.) Are you investing in their natural education and other extracurricular activities which would include sports for both males and females?

Mothers, stay very prayerful as I open the following discussion. Take care not to make your little one more precious than Jesus. Yes, I said it. This is a huge world, and they must be adequately prepared to assume their rightful role. They might be the center of your life, but believe me, others will not accept them as such. They are part of the melting pot and sometimes—based on their behavior that has been allowed and accepted by you—will prevent them from melting within the society. Great care must be taken that they do not become selfish, self-centered, or manipulative. These behaviors are exhibited also in children from two-parent homes, but I am specifically addressing single mothers. Children learn at early stages how to get what they want. They will also put you on a guilt trip, so they can have their way. Watch out for these as well. You cannot and should not go overboard with your child, especially those of you with only one child. That little girl may be ever so beautiful in your eyes, but she may not be that to others. Do not spoil and give in to her every wish and whim. Real life is coming at some point in her life, and she must know she cannot get whatever she wishes whenever she speaks it. There must be a balance.

The same goes for those with that only boy. He must learn to accept responsibility, love and respect his mother. He is not so handsome that he cannot get his precious hands dirty in taking out the garbage. Likewise, do not spoil him, waiting on him all the time (age appropriately). Only children either male or female must be assigned household chores with the expectation of completing the tasks as expected. Love them appropriately as a parent. They are humans with a sinful nature, so take that wall down that "my child would never do such things." Your child will lie just like another if it will get them out of trouble. It is okay to say *no* to your child without feeling guilty.

Communicate with them on an ongoing basis, so you will know how they feel about certain issues. In today's society, it is imperative that you really know what your child is doing on their iPad especially as it relates to social media. They need to know you love them.

Openly discuss their relationships with friends. Let them know there is no subject off the table. If you have boys, it would be beneficial if you had a positive male who can talk with your son as he enters puberty and manhood. (If the father is available, hopefully, he can address this area.) Not every man in the church can help in this area, so please, be prayerful if the father isn't available.

Men are the heads, but they must be taught. Being the head doesn't mean dictating orders while others watch. There are a number of responsibilities a male child should be taught, one of which includes household chores. These responsibilities must be introduced during their early years and maintained/continued as they mature. With each stage of development and maturity; additional responsibilities should be added. You are the mother, but please, do not be their "maid." How will they know they can perform if the opportunities are not provided? Growing up, especially teenage years, is the time for them to show you they know how to be responsible. This responsibility is not limited to doing their schoolwork but also household chores, church affiliations, and others.

As a result of today's multimedia, it is critical that you seek to develop children that are spiritually and mentally healthy as they face the many tricks that they must encounter. They should be taught the truth of God's Word with understanding. Knowing that God is and will always be the supreme and Holy God is foremost.

Cyberbullying is a strong trick from the devil. I often ponder why someone would commit suicide because someone on a computer tells you to do so. Children today are so gullible. You must monitor this behavior and affirm your love for them. A part of parenting is developing self-assured, positive, self-esteemed individuals. This is mastered in how we live and teach our children daily. None of this can happen in a year's time but, rather, in parenting daily. There are numerous books written on how and the best ways of parenting, but it is only in the implementation by the parent will it come to light.

The Bible says in Proverbs 22:6, "Train up a child in the way he should go: and when he is old, he will not depart from it." Training is continuous beginning at birth. It is during this training process that you can correct certain behaviors. Remember your childhood as you endeavor to raise your child. There were certainly things you did that your parents did not like. Now, what about reaping and sowing? If you gave your parents a hard time in certain situations, just remember you are reaping. You can handle it with the help of the Lord and the patience He will give you along the way.

Correction in their training is needful. It is your duty to correct, chaste, punish, and when necessary, spank/whip your child. I worked for IDCFS, and the law does not say you cannot punish your child. You cannot inflict bruises upon your child. I will add that some things parents did in the past were abusive like the use of ironing chords, sticks, tree branches, and the like were awful, but we now must abide by the law of the land. The parent should be smarter than the child; therefore, you must learn what really hurts the most. Sometimes, that whipping really hurt, but it did not deter that behavior. You must learn what impacts that child the most and use that method. Take away the cell phone, video games, etc. completely for a week, month, or longer if needed. Once you have established a punishment time period, do not give in. Be consistent and persistent; do not be moved by their cries or pleas.

Parents, stop trying to give them everything you can think of to make up for the missing father. Tangible things cannot nor will ever be able to replace a real father's love. Buying those expensive clothes or huge birthday party you cannot afford. Who are you really trying to impress? Children grow so very fast so why spend one hundred dollars on a pair of gym shoes that will last for only a few months. (Why don't you open a college savings account?) Now, if you are financially fixed, then, go ahead, but if not, get wise. Learn where to go to get these high-end items for low end costs. (Stop trying to impress folks.) Make sure your children are always clean and neat and teach them the importance of life's basic principles.

All children (boys and girls) should learn how to cook and clean. They should learn the importance of proper grooming. Do not allow your children to go unkempt and disheveled because they choose to ignore your rules. Consistency is important. Some children, for whatever reason, will try to get away without taking a bath, but it is your responsibility to make sure it happens. No one wants to sit by someone with a bad odor; personal hygiene must be stressed until they get the point. Make sure their clothing is clean. Now, this might become problematic as they get older, but remember, you are the parent and they are the child. This child is representing you; therefore, do not allow them to go out of the house looking any strange kind of way. You are also imparting important life rules for them to continue and, hopefully, teach their children. It might not be possible for you to indulge them with the latest of fashions, but they can learn how to take care of what they possess.

Please recognize that there are some things your child may not be ready to receive because they are not mature or responsible enough. It should not matter that your child's friend has an iPhone and other expensive items; if you cannot afford it, then, the answer is *no*! Live within your means, and let the child know the truth—I cannot afford it right now. This would be an excellent opportunity to teach them the value of establishing a savings account to get that special item. Mothers, if you celebrate Christmas, do not get into unnecessary debt for one day. Be wise!

To those mothers that had children out of wedlock or bad divorces, stop talking negatively about the father because your relationship went sour. Reality check: you were the one who engaged intimately with that man for those moments of pleasure to conceive. Okay, he left and does doesn't want a relationship with you. Do not punish the child/children and deny them the opportunity to knowing their father. Every child needs a father in their lives. If the father is willing and available, plan for visits to take place on regular basis. If he chooses not to be involved, then do not force the matter, but still, don't talk negatively about him to the children. They will develop their own opinion as they mature and age-appropriate conversations take place. It would be advisable to seek a positive line of communication with his relatives. Most grandmothers love their grandchildren and want to spend time with them. Child support is needed, but again, don't hold the child hostage because of the negative actions of the father or mother.

It is critical that you watch your behavior toward your child/children during your periods of being upset or angry, especially after a difficult day at work or unfruitful conversation with the father. Do not take it out on the children and express wishing they were never born. Please, do not scold the child unnecessarily when they have done nothing wrong because his or her looks reminds you of the father. The child/children should look like the father or other of his relatives but don't punish the child. A saying from my mother, we (the child) did not ask to be born. Get to know his family, and remember, everything in your family is not so great either.

Loving your child is critical and sets the stage for them being able to navigate through life. Showing your love is beyond giving them tangible things. They need to hear meaningful "I love you" on a regular basis. Children need a balanced, disciplined, and consistent loving life. Research has been conducted that supports children, especially adolescents, desire to be disciplined. Boundaries must be set that are clear. Your house rules should not be dictated by what friends' parents allow. Good parenting standards have been around for years, and believe me, they still work in today's society.

Technology cannot replace parenting. Your established rules and regulations should be adhered to, or they suffer the consequences. Do not talk empty threats. Living in this modern society does not declare children rule. They are still children and must be taught. Along this same line, allow your child to be a child. They are not adults and should not be treated, dressed, or communicated with in such a manner. I do not mean you should baby them but keep them in their age category. They might be knowledgeable in some areas, but that does not denote you should give them a responsibility beyond their age comprehension. For example, a nine-year-old should not be expected to stay home alone nor babysit their siblings for extended hours or prepare the family dinner. Supervision is important.

I would caution you regarding leaving an irresponsible teenager home alone with their siblings for extended periods of time. You are the parent and must not relinquish your parenting role on your children. This includes being careful regarding asking them their opinions concerning critical house matters. Always know who and where your children are visiting. Beware of those overnight sleepovers. You know who is coming in your home but have no control over someone else's.

When your children are older and travel away from home, get those apps for their phones that always allows you to track their every move and location. These are a must in the world we are living.

Accept the role as a parent, and do not give this responsibility to another. It is not the responsibility of the grandparent to raise your child if you are capable. Do not look at this portion of your life as dull and uneventful or meaningless. They will grow up and be out of the house at some point in time. Raise them to the best of your ability with the help of God to become competent and reliable adults. Children are our heritage, and we should leave a positive legacy that they will remember and pass on to their children. Remember, your child/children are very important but should not be your entire life. You must take care of yourself, because one day, they will grow up and leave the nest.

Just because you are the sole parent in the house should not mean others (father, grandparents, church members, etc.) cannot assist in raising your children to become healthy adults. It is imperative that you know the people your child spends a substantial amount of time with. (Yes, there are child molesters in the church building and family so take extreme caution.) Beware of those overnight activities. In fact, today, you might want to eliminate such activities. Now, you want your child to be well-rounded, so try not to be such a worrier that you do not allow them to go on activities with their friends. It is a good idea for them to get involved in sports, music, girl or boy scouts because it will broaden their perspective of life from another angle. If your church does not have children activities and clubs, then this might be an opportunity for you to establish something.

Remember, when you were younger and said you would never do your child in such a manner, stop and really look at what you are doing. Face it, we become our parents in many aspects, or we go the other extremes and overindulge our children with things we were not able to obtain while growing up. If you are the sole source of income, you cannot provide the child with everything. Stay within your financial means, or you will, then, be saddled with the burden to trying to get out of debt. You cannot be all things to your child, and you must face that fact. Whatever happened to having ice cream and cake for a birthday party? Why would you spend hundreds of dollars at your expense at a "famous eatery?" It would be wise to save money for their high school and college graduation, so they can have a great time of their choice. Missionary Lila Mitchell was famous for quoting if we deny something from our children because it is against the "church rule," we should be found giving them an equally pleasing alternative. Plan for those developmental milestones that will come.

Talk with your child/children on a regular basis. Establish and maintain family time for everyone to come together and just talk. Don't let the technology of today separate you because everyone is doing their own thing. Have family outings and trips. Take a vacation together and make sure they are part of the planning. You don't have a mate, but you do have children, and they require your attention. If they are involved in sports or other school activities, make sure you are present. (Yes, even if it is on a service night.) They need your in-person support.

As your child/children get older, have some real heart-to-heart conversations with them about life. If you had them out of wedlock, it is imperative that you share your love for them. It is all right to discuss the value of a father in the home as they plan their future. This would be the point of stressing integrity to either your son or daughter.

Sex is a topic that should be directly and honestly discussed. While the children are young, teach them the correct names of their anatomy rather than "worldly name." The vagina is a vagina and not a pocketbook or cookie. (This was something I learned while working as a sex abuse investigator.) Let them know that having children is an at least eighteen-year binding legal responsibility. Sons must know there is great value and responsibility in fathering a child. Conversations regarding homosexuality should be discussed from the biblical perspective. Let them know this is wrong and will never be right in the sight of God. Give it to them straight that two males nor two females cannot reproduce, and this was never intended by God. Discuss what the world is permitting is not ordained of God, especially marriage. Stress we must love the person but not their behavior.

This is another reason to know who is in the households when your children go for overnight sleepovers. Face the fact that some families should be listed as off limits. Child molesters are cunning and crafty people and know how to entice children. Please note that many of these people are not strangers. Yes, we have family members that are homosexuals even if we do not want to acknowledge their sexual preference. Keep your children away from negative environments as much as possible. Sisters, sisters, if your church allows dating, please be prayerful. If you are sanctified, kissing and hugging should not be on the agenda. Doing so will stir some emotions that might be very difficult to halt. Both of you might be clean but you don't want to get wrinkled either. I would suggest go out in groups.

Don't become so needy that you are seeing multiple brothers, and do not allow them into your home. Meet with them on the outside until that "one" asks for your hand in marriage, and it would be at that point you introduce him to the children. If the children know the brother, please be cautious of his interactions with the children. Watch closely and monitor any relationships that may be developing between your children and the brother. Be careful of his giving your children gifts all the time, etc. If God is not telling you he is your husband, maintain a "distance." Do not allow yourself to get too comfortable or familiar with him. I would hope that you are not just going out with a brother just to be going out. Please, go out in a group. It is important that you not let your good be evil spoken. You are setting an example before your children. Don't use your children as bait to get a husband, and don't let the brother get to you through your children. Don't get to the point where you feel needy and settle for someone that may be using your children as bait to get in your home.

I will also add that it might not be such a good idea to allow them to visit where there are no rules or guidelines. If they allow their children to do things you are not in agreement with, then, let your precious ones remain with you. Remember, your rules are yours, and you demand obedience. Don't be a hypocrite. Your child will tell on you when least expected.

Satisfied

Have you ever thought the reason you are not satisfied is because you are so busy looking at someone or something else? Satisfied is defined as: (1) to put an end to (a desire, want, need, etc.) by sufficient or ample provision; (2) to fulfill the desires, expectations, needs, or demands of (a person, the mind, etc.) to give full contentment to; (3) pleased and contented; and (4) fully gratified.

Now, Scripture uses the word "content," to make satisfied, gratify. "But godliness with contentment is great gain" (1 Timothy 6:6). Just looking and digesting this Scripture alone lets you know that having God brings and gives us a tremendous satisfaction of security that everything is all right or going to be all right.

Philippians. 4:11 declares, "Not that I spoke of want: for I have learned in whatsoever state I am, therewith to be content." Repeat this scripture aloud and listen to the words. It is telling you to be content or better yet, satisfied with your current situation. Work within your realm of singleness and refrain from looking at others or things beyond your means. Sometimes, we complain about not having a spouse, but I think the problem is deeper. If we really look introspectively, we would see that there is personal dissatisfaction going on and believe someone else can fix it, or at least, it can be covered up. We complain about not having any clothes to wear, yet we have a closet full. We don't like the shape of our bodies, so we go to the gym and workout or, better still, take a pill to lose weight. Our hair just won't act right, so we buy a wig or weave. Nobody likes us, so we sit in a corner and never make a move to talk with anyone, or you could be one who wants to monopolize every conversation; therefore, when people see you coming, they go the other way. We are fearfully and wonderfully made, so stop complaining about you. Rather than looking at the glass as half empty, look at it as being half full. Look at yourself more from positive aspects. You have some great abilities; explore them.

In your reaching a level of satisfaction, you must find other creative ways of living your own personal "purpose-filled" life as a single sister. In recognition of your purpose, you will reach the conclusion without hesitation that you are living for Christ. In living for Christ, you want to make sure your life is filled with those things that please Him. You are living, not existing. You should want to leave a legacy. Christ is the head of our lives and He must be first. We should always acknowledge Him to lead, guide and direct our path.

What is your purpose for being single? What are you doing to enhance and make your life rich? Stop! Be quiet! Listen to what the Spirit is saying to you. Stop the nonsense thinking and admit you are in a great place, and God has been better than good to you. Stop entertaining the devil and put away the pity parties. Stop putting yourself down. Be quiet. God wants to give you an injection of spiritual Holy Ghost anesthesia. He knows you need to relax your spiritual mind, so He can talk to you. Be quiet and accept your adrenaline tablets. You may need to take them every hour for a month based on your current situation. This is no time to ignore or turn a deaf ear to God. You know the voice of God. Let the Spirit calm all those fears and uncertainties.

Lamentations 3:26 lets us know: "It is good that a man should both hope and quietly wait for the salvation of the Lord." The devil will never tell you to invest in the work of the Lord because he knows the great blessings you will receive. Finally, now that you are calm and afresh in the spirit, you can listen with a pure heart to what the Lord is saying. Your heart (mind) is open and receptive. You can hear His voice clearly now. "Stand up, My daughter, and go forth in the work I have given unto you." Do not be afraid of the faces because God will strengthen you step by step during your journey. He will never leave nor forsake us.

There is a place of rest. Psalm 37:7 clearly declares, "Rest in the Lord, and wait patiently for Him." This is referring strictly to waiting on the Lord and not any human. It is so important to be "in the Lord" and not on the surface. Get out of the boat at this point of your life and get wet, drenched in the Holy Ghost and love of the Almighty God. If we are not in the water, He cannot carry us to the next level in Him. When Peter asked Jesus to allow him to come unto Him on the water, Jesus replied, "Come." Have you asked God for that rest—that peace—that can only come from Him? If you have asked, do not be like Peter once you are out there, begin to look around at your situation as the devil has painted. Look solely at Jesus and think peace and quiet. "Great peace have they which love thy law: and nothing shall offend them" (Psalm 119:165).

Moving along to Hebrews 13:5, "Let your conversation be without covetousness; and be content with such things as ye have; for He hath said, I will never leave thee, nor forsake thee." It is very important that single sisters refrain from being in ongoing company of married sisters. Face the fact; married sisters generally talk about their husbands and children. Those married sisters are going to boast on their husband and rightfully so, but I am not interested in the "my husband this and my husband that" whether it is good or bad. Likewise, it is uncomfortable listening to a wife constantly complaining about her husband knowing she is not about to leave him. I know some people need a sounding board, but this is not the sound I desire to hear. It is sad to say but, if you offered advise they would not take it.

Single sisters our conversations, most of the time, should be centered on working and moving in the Lord. Has God given you any new ideas or revelations of His Word? Have you gotten any ideas on how to bring more souls to Christ? What about taking a trip with other single sisters to a place you have never visited? What about volunteering at a women's shelter? The lists goes on and on. God ends this verse with, "I will never leave thee, nor forsake thee." What more comforting words could be said about our current plight in life? God is there all the time. He is the comfort of all comforts. Let's keep the conversation on God and pleasant things edifying to single sisters. By the way, do not bring up the boyfriends from the past; watch the mind.

My mother would often tell me that I was a single birth, so I need to journey alone. Now, I may be alone, but I am not alone. I have the Holy Ghost abiding on the inside, and when encouragement is needed, it comes. We are not always in the spirit, so what are you doing for the natural woman? How are you filling your days and nights when not in church service or other activities? Who are your friends? What do you enjoy doing? How do you generally spend your leisure time? It is time to come out, come out from wherever you are and wake up.

Time is far spent; shift your focus. You have gone too long in the same frame of mind. Your mind and spirit must come to rest that I am satisfied with not having a companion. I can shop, travel, read a book, look at a movie, and most of all, go to heaven without a husband. Yes, I am satisfied. No, I am not broken. The only fixing I need to do is staying prepared to fight the good fight of faith. I can rest knowing that I am doing the will of Him that has called me out of a world of sin and shame. I know in whom I trust and believe. I am more than a conqueror because God is on my side. Yes, I am satisfied, and there is no shame or other reproach upon me.

"But godliness with contentment is great gain" (1 Timothy 6:6). Now, this is where God wants you in Him. Once you reach this level of satisfaction in God, the worldly desires are no longer in the picture. It is not until we get in that secret place with God can we reach a level of fulfillment and satisfaction. If we spend most of our energies doing the will of God, everything else will fall into place. Our thoughts will be centered on what, how, and when we can continue to do our assigned work for the Lord. We are only on this Earth for a specific number of years. What are you spending your day doing? It cannot nor should it be complaining about not being married. There are so many other things that you should be focused upon. Settle yourself. Contentment is satisfaction; settle in where you are without any of the ifs, ands, or buts.

God doesn't want you to be one of those multitaskers that never get anything accomplished. Doing many things and mastering nothing is not good. Sometimes, if you have several things to do, one will get messed up. So just think about it. God wants total focus. He wants perfected, single, sold-out sister that does His work without excuse. The reward is great, and you have already received benefits of God blessing you. Relax now and just float in the love, peace, and joy in God during this season. Right now, what God has for you is singleness. It is not a bad thing.

My sisters, let's get to the point that the married sisters will envy (spiritually) us for our move in the Lord. Let them see the glow we wear because of the hours we can spend with God and the illumination we receive. Let our projects and works to help others be noised abroad. Let our good works as a single sister become a banner for the younger generation of sisters, so they will begin to plan more on enjoying a single life rather than looking at wedding dresses and talking about having babies. Let our little girls see that we are okay being without a husband because we have houses, cars, great jobs, beautiful clothes, and the anointing of God upon us.

Please yourself to a fault. Older people make bucket lists which is nothing more than a list of dreams and desires. Take the time to sit down and make your personal list. What is your most desired dream? Is it traveling to a certain place? Do you want to own your own home or purchase that dream automobile? Do you want to establish that agency or company to help the elderly, young or poor? Is it your dream or desire? Now is your chance. Take a few moments to list them in order of priority and some research might be required. Finance is generally involved in most of our endeavors so begin planning and prioritizing to meet those goals. A trip anywhere in America is doable if you would only plan. Get that passport if you have dreams of traveling beyond the United States of America. Get at least one credit card that you can use for travel purposes only. If you enjoy dressing, then shop until you drop. Always look your best. Go buy that fur. In fact, buy two if you can afford to do it. Watch yourself now. Don't get high-minded because you can afford to shop at will. In fact, give some of those outfits you no longer wear that are in excellent condition to another sister.

Let's live the life in spirit and truth. Final Scripture of the book comes from Hebrews 4:12: "For the word of God is quick, and powerful, and sharper than any two-edged sword, piercing even to the dividing asunder of soul and spirit, and of the joints and marrow, and is a discerner of the thoughts and intents of the heart." So in simple, plain, everyday words, you can't fool God. He knows your thoughts. He knows when you really are satisfied or just faking to get by.

As you really investigate your life and are not satisfied, what and how do you think another person can provide that satisfaction? We must be pleased with ourselves first. I dare you to stand in the mirror and compliment yourself. This is not bragging. If you don't think you are brilliant in some areas, don't expect others to do it for you. Yes! We could have always done better in some areas, but let's move forward. Take some time right now and make a list of your good qualities. What things do you excel in and have a passion for doing? What are those things that really make you happy? Why aren't you doing more in that area? It is time to work and stop wasting time; Jesus is coming soon. Will Jesus find you working or pinning?

I am at peace with my singleness. Yes, it took me some years to face reality and do what the Lord wanted me to do. I am saddened as I look back at the years I wasted in selfishness that could have been used for God. But God knows, and I thank Him for the opportunity to write this book and pray it is of consolation and help to others. God cannot be a husband to us, but He most certainly is the best, the greatest Father, Counselor, Provider, and Friend. God can *out-provide* any "man." Therefore, be satisfied that you have the greatest without measure.

Words cannot describe how I feel about my status today. I really wish I had been told to change my focus years ago and really enjoy singleness. There is a satisfaction and peace that all my sisters should be relishing that has been taken away. We have such a great wealth of knowledge that should be shared with others in the further of the Gospel and other positives things of life. Let's keep this door open and begin to teach others the importance of reaching their personal self-potential. There is greatness in each of us, and it is up to us to let it out.

As I conclude writing, God has not given me the slightest glimpse into my future. Life should not be on hold because you are waiting for a prophecy to come into existence. There are television and Facebook announcements of couples marrying later in life, and these are, again, so touching. Despite these and other news commentaries that I may view in the days ahead, I can assure you that I am not sitting pinning away in despair. I have great contentment and satisfaction in knowing I have weathered many storms in life with the help of God. It has not been a cake walk in my forty years in holiness, but it has been a fantastic life, and I would not take anything back. It has been a learning experience that I hope to be able to share with others, especially those that are single and feel they are in despair. Look up and live, my sisters. The sun is shining, and God is smiling upon you.

In writing this book, I referred to Kenneth as the "love of my life," but guess what? I really found the love of my life in 1978 at the Fifth Street Church of God. I found someone that showed me an everlasting love. Someone who forgave me when I faltered; someone who loved me for me. The love of my life is Jesus Christ who bore my sins on Calvary. The love of my life that calmed many seas during those unspeakable stormy days. The love of my life opened doors that I didn't know existed or would ever come into being. The love of my life who has comforted me during so many midnight seasons when the tears of sorrow flooded by pillows. The love of my life that doesn't lie. The love of my life that is dependable. The love of my life that fulfills His promises. The love of my life who will answer before I call. The love of my life who knows the very desires of my heart. The love of my life lifted me when I was in a horrible pit of self-pity. The love of my life gave me health when the doctor diagnosed me with cancer. The love my life has filled me and is allowing me to experience the greatest spiritual joy I never realized or thought would happen. The love of my life that has opened doors and windows that were nonexistent. The love of my life who has entrusted me to write this book. The love of my life is imparting more and more of His Spirit into me through His Word, and I am ever grateful and indebted.

Jesus has done things for me that no man could have ever done. I appreciate the love of my life and have made a vow that I will do the work He has sent me to do. I am so satisfied with my life.

The love of my life is Jesus, the sweetest name on Earth. The love of my life can be yours too. I am willing to share. The door is open, won't you come?

Single!
Sanctified!
Satisfied!

CPSIA information can be obtained
at www.ICGtesting.com
Printed in the USA
LVHW041443120920
665568LV00005B/6

9 781644 681466